A HARVEST

LOVE

A HARVEST OF LOVE

Tools to Cultivate the Fruit of the Spirit

REBEKAH MONTGOMERY

PROMISE
PRESS
An Imprint of Barbour Publishing

Published by Promise Press, an imprint of Barbour Publishing, Inc., P.O. Box 719, Uhrichsville, Ohio 44683 http://www.barbourbooks.com

Member of the
Evangelical Christian
Publishers Association

Printed in the United States of America.

Foreword

I enjoy flowers of all description—except plastic. To me there is something offensive about transforming soft, fragrant petals into sticky plastic—but I thoroughly delight in the real items. Fresh-cut flowers fill my house with fragrance, but what I enjoy even more are plants that bloom outside in the spring and then continue to blossom inside. When the icy winds turn the prairie flowers into pale gold drifts, when everything seems dead, these flowers wait safely indoors with me. Their cheeks pressed against the windows, they watch for signs of spring's return, when we all can go outside into the sunshine again.

In my quest for flowers, I often "force" spring-blooming bulbs. I wait until the very end of the planting season when the bulbs are marked down, and then I buy cheap, leftover crocus, tulips, paper-whites, or smaller daffodil bulbs. They wait patiently in a paper bag in the produce compartment of my refrigerator for about forty-five days, more or less. In mid-January, when I am trapped indoors by ice, snow, and subzero temperatures, when the world outside looks like a black-and-white TV with bad static, I plant the bulbs in my collection of interesting pots.

Then comes the fun! In the warmth of the house, the bulbs come up very quickly. Every day they get taller, and then one exciting day there is a blush of color on the buds. Then blooms! Color! Sweet fragrance! (All except the paper-whites. They look pretty, but they smell like, well, I have to admit it—cat urine—so I set them in a well-ventilated spot.) In winter's cold, dead world, my home is filled with amazing spring while I await the real thing.

God's miraculous love for us is very much like these vest-pocket, indoor garden patches. The world is caught in a deep freeze of sin. The cold is so cruel it will murder our souls. But dormant within us is sweet-smelling life, planted by God's hand when we were yet in our mothers' wombs. Either the Spirit of God will awaken that life—or sin's deep chill will kill it.

Christ gave up His human wants and wishes to be obedient to death on the cross, and in the same way we surrender our will to Christ. Like a bulb planted in the ground, when we give our lives to Christ, we are buried with Him. We die to ourselves so we can live for God.

Then the miracle takes place! God's Holy Spirit stirs our souls, awakening it so it can grow to new heights. That particle of life planted in us long ago by the hand of God responds to the warmth of His love. Miraculously, our souls change from unsightly bulbs to fragrant flowers, transformed by His love.

But this is just the beginning. As we respond to God's love, we will become more like Him. The metamorphosis will continue, until the love of God wafts out from our souls with the sweet fragrance of selfless love. God's love will enable us to love others as Christ did—gently, purely, and eternally.

Make no mistake, though: Many so-called Christians are no more concerned with loving God with all their heart, soul, and mind than a dyed-in-the-wool heathen. Nor are they interested in loving their neighbors as themselves. Their lives are all about them and what they want. You might say these are the plastic flowers in the garden of life; they may *look* remarkably real, but they lack the essence of life that makes flowers beautiful. We need to make sure we are not one of those.

Other Christian believers are only marginally interested in loving either God or their fellow human beings. Unfortunately, in one way or another, we all fall into this category, because sin constantly batters and blights our souls. That's why we need to yield our lives to the work of the Master Gardener.

Unlike a tulip bulb that calmly and willingly accepts whatever I do to it, we have a disconcerting habit of resisting God. Should a flower bulb argue vehemently with me about where I proposed to plant it, or if it dug itself back out of the soil, I would simply discard it. Fortunately, God in His gracious mercy has far more patience with us. His patience stems from His great love.

In a cold, dark, love-starved world, our conversion from bulb to bloom is a sign of God's power and love. It is like a welcome mat to those around us, an invitation to inhale God's love and be healed. As we accept the Master Gardener's work in our hearts, our lives become a brilliant witness to God's transforming love. Because of the sweet fragrance of love that emanates from our lives, the world will know we are God's.

Chapter 1

Love—God's Style
Identifying the True Vine and Fruit

David had so much on his mind he couldn't sleep. As he paced on the balcony outside his luxurious house, he gazed up at the stars and prayed for help and wisdom. He had a close relationship with God, and his heart thrilled as he talked to Him where he could see the temporary temple environs as well as the glory of the sky.

With his prayer still on his lips, a torchlight procession caught his eye. He saw a young maiden and her servants in the temple's Court of the Women, moving toward the ritual baths. David knew that devout women took a monthly bath to declare themselves ritually clean before they took part in any temple function. No doubt this young woman was about to do the same. When she entered the little bathhouse tent that was constructed without a roof, he had a perfect view of what was about to take place.

David knew he should avert his eyes. But he also knew that the young woman thought no one could see her, and the temptation to watch her was great. . . .

She opened her robes and slid her simple white tunic to the floor. . . .

By the time she immersed herself in the bath, David knew he had to have her.

Before his affair with her was over, he would commit adultery, murder, bury a son, and see his family torn apart because of his illicit desire. Some would call the saga of David and Bathsheba a love story, but that would be a mistake. Real love, the sort given to us by the Author of Love, is about giving, not taking. David merely took. In reality, his feelings were the opposite of true love.

False Vines, Poisonous Fruit

"I was fourteen when I got pregnant with my first child. I just wanted someone to love me."

"We're in love but we want to live together for a while to

make sure."

"We got a divorce because our love just died. It was no one's fault."

These sorts of references to love are all too common in our world today. Love may be the greatest force in the world, but it's also the most misused, misunderstood, and misappropriated word in the English language. Proffered like Sleeping Beauty's poisonous apple, it is used to describe lust, sex, appetite, romance, and a dizzying variety of inanities like these: "I love chocolate." "I love cats." "I love coral pink." "I love clean sheets on the clothesline." These may all be nice, fuzzy feelings—but none of them bear any resemblance to true love.

You'd think we would be sick of the word *love*. Instead, far from being satiated by the word's frequent use, humans everywhere are starving for true love; in fact, we're in the midst of an appalling famine. People search longingly and desperately for love's sweet fruits. Rather than go without, these people accept artificial, wax fruit varieties in lieu of the genuine, nourishing article. They primp, diet, and submit to radical surgery, all in the hopes of planting fertile seeds of love in their lives. All they end up with are sterile vines.

No matter how hard we work to gain love, all our efforts will be unsuccessful; nothing we can do will ever buy us love. The sixties' radicals were right after all: Love is free. Through no merit of our own, true love is served to our hungry hearts from Christ's bleeding hands.

True biblical love is a simple concept but impossible to grasp without the indwelling of the Holy Spirit. In the same way that poisonous inky caps are often mistaken for edible field mushrooms, sometimes we may mistake for love a shriveled-up weed of self-interest growing in the stagnant swamps of our hearts. But there is no replacement for the transforming Seed of God, planted by the Holy Spirit in good soil and watered by the Living Water; there are only artificial substitutes that are often deadly.

Most individuals measure their own worthiness by the quality of other people's love for them, but God measures our worth by His love for us. We pass His love on to those around us when we love others as we love ourselves. The miracle of God's transforming power is the only way to find the rare and fragrant blooms of true love.

Fertilize Your Mind
What God Means When He Commands, "Love."

Compassion: A feeling of deep sympathy and sorrow for someone who is stricken by suffering or misfortune, accompanied by a strong desire to alleviate the cause.

Pity: Sympathetic or kindly sorrow excited by the suffering or misfortune of another, often leading one to give relief or aid or to show mercy.

Charity: Charitable actions such as almsgiving or performing other benevolent actions of any sort for the needy with no expectation of material reward for one's service.

Agape: 1. The love of God for humanity. 2. The spiritual love of one Christian for another, corresponding to the love of God for human beings.

Although We Have Weeds, God Loves Us

Remember the story Jesus told about the Prodigal Son? No matter how much the son hurt the father, the father still welcomed him back with open arms.

God loves us the same way. No matter how far we run from Him, no matter how much we hurt Him, whenever we turn back toward our home with Him, He comes running out to meet us, His arms held out in love. That is the way true love acts.

The Prodigal College Student

On a savagely cold winter day in the Midwest, Charles and Carlene learned that one of their sons, Doug, was missing from college.

"We got a letter from Doug in the mail. In it, he said he didn't have enough money to attend the next semester, so he was going to hitchhike to New York City," said Charles. "What he didn't know was this: On the dean's desk was a letter granting him a full scholarship for the next semester!"

Doug's letter went on to say he was going to try to break into show business, because many people had told him he was handsome enough to be a Broadway star.

Said Carlene: "When I read his letter, I nearly died! I knew how cold it was outside. If he didn't get a ride, he might freeze to death. I also knew Doug was kind of naïve—some pervert or murderer might pick him up! And he didn't have much money. What was he going to eat? Where was he going to sleep?

"My emotions were torn in two ways: I was so angry at

him for doing this lamebrain thing where he could get himself hurt or killed—and at the same time, I wanted him in my arms so I could hold him and know that he was all right."

Charles and Carlene notified the state police, but the telephone was heartbreakingly silent for the next several weeks. Doug seemed to have simply disappeared off the face of the earth. Carlene and Charles contemplated driving the highways to search for him.

"Our whole family and church were praying for his safety. Carlene and I barely slept at night for the horror of what could happen to him," said Charles. "We could only put our fears in God's hands and trust Him to look after our boy."

The nagging worries tormented them until one day out of the blue a postcard appeared. The canceled stamp read "Raleigh, South Carolina."

"Too cold in New York," said the card. "Takes a while to be a star. Headed south. Having fun. Love, Doug."

"I laughed, then I cried," said Carlene. "I was relieved to know he was alive, but frightened to death that he was still hitchhiking."

For the next several months, random cards appeared, postmarked from various cities all over the South. The cards never gave much information, just verified that Doug was apparently alive and well.

Then one spring day came the knock on the door. Charles

and Carlene opened it, and there stood Doug, tanned, taller, and a lot thinner.

"It was the classic Prodigal Son story. All the worry he put us through was forgiven and forgotten when we saw him," said Charles. "While we didn't kill the fatted calf, we did grill steaks. And I gained a greater understanding of how much God the Father loves us. Although we've made a mess of our lives and caused our heavenly Father pain, He still welcomes us with open arms when we return to Him."

Jesus Is Love—Identifying the True Vine

The ultimate description of love is in 1 Corinthians 13. As you read through this passage, you will be struck by the resemblance between these verses and Jesus' life. In fact, everywhere that you read the word "love," substitute "Jesus." You will see that His name fits comfortably within the text; that's because He is the personification of love.

The tragedy is that we can't read those same verses and honestly substitute our own names. How far short we fall of the way God intended us to love.

Plant the Seeds of True Love

If I speak in the tongues of men and of angels, but have not love, I am only a resounding gong or a clanging cymbal. If I have the gift of prophecy and can fathom all mysteries and all knowledge, and if I have a faith that can move mountains, but have not love, I am nothing. If I give all I possess to the poor and surrender my body to the flames, but have not love, I gain nothing.

Love is patient, love is kind. It does not envy, it does not boast, it is not proud. It is not rude, it is not self-seeking, it is not easily angered, it keeps no record of wrongs. Love does not delight in evil but rejoices with the truth. It always protects, always trusts, always hopes, always perseveres.

Love never fails. But where there are prophecies, they will cease; where there are tongues, they will be stilled; where there is knowledge, it will pass away. For we know in part and we prophesy in part, but when perfection comes, the imperfect disappears. When I was a child, I talked like a child, I thought like a child, I reasoned like a child. When I became a man, I put childish ways behind me. Now we see but a poor reflection as in a mirror; then we shall see face to face. Now I know in part; then I shall know fully, even as I am fully known.

And now these three remain: faith, hope and love.
But the greatest of these is love.

1 CORINTHIANS 13 NIV
THE LOVE CHAPTER

This Scripture passage describes pure love, what it is and what it is not. The Bible also says that love is the fruit of the Spirit in our lives (Galatians 5:22). In other words, the kind of love described in 1 Corinthians 13 will only appear in a life willingly connected to the Holy Spirit, one that allows Him to grow in it.

If you only memorize one chapter in the Bible, make it 1 Corinthians 13. As you commit this chapter to memory, heed its words and ask the Holy Spirit to make it real in your life. It will change you—eternally!

Are You a Fruitful Vine or a Sterile Weed? How Will People Know?

In a world of counterfeit Christians, do people recognize you as Christ's disciple? Do they know you are a follower of Christ because you say you are? Because you sing in the choir? Because you are a preacher? Or Sunday school teacher? Or is everyone in your family Christians, so you are too? Do people around you say, "He must be a Christian because he goes to church"? Or "She's a Christian because she doesn't have any vices"? Do they think you're a Christian because of the way you dress? Because of your political affiliations or beliefs?

Jesus said that everyone would recognize His followers because of their love.

How do people know that you are a follower of Christ?

The ability to love
as described in 1 Corinthians 13
may have to be forcibly learned
by a deliberate act
of the will with the aid
of the Holy Spirit.

CARL V. BINKLEY

The Fruit of Those Planted in Christ

Sound biblical doctrine is important—but loving the heretic and sinner is far more important than correcting him. By the same token, Jesus did not say, "People will know you're a follower of Mine if you can explain complicated theological treatises or work amazing miracles." Instead He said, "By this shall all men know that ye are my disciples, if ye have love one to another" (John 13:35).

- A fruitful believer's constant prayer will be, "Fill me with Your supernatural love."

- An effective Sunday school teacher's prayer of preparation will be, "Love my students through me."

- A successful parent's prayer will be, "Help my children to better understand You through my love."

- The prayer of the believing child will be, "Let me lovingly respect my parents."

- The Christian husband's prayer will be, "Show me how to love my wife as much as I love my own body."

- A Christian wife's prayer will be, "Give me the ability to love my husband with respect, giving myself to him."

- The prayer of a God-fearing employee will be, "Let me serve my employer with a heart of love; let me love my fellow workers so that they may see You."

- The prayer of the believing employer will be, "Let me show my employees Christ through my love for them."

- The prayer of the oppressed will be, "Let me love those who misuse me."

- The prayer of the powerful will be, "Let me love with all my power."

Doctrine has splintered the church into more than 450 denominations, each believing its interpretation of the Bible is more correct than the next. And because each believes its doctrine more pure, it can't join with the others, let alone love one another or serve with one another.

[These biblical] interpretations divide rather than bring unity and cause men to wonder who is a true follower of Christ.

CARL V. BINKLEY

Love is often a one-way street—all giving and not receiving. It doesn't always seem fair, does it? But this is the kind of love God has for us.

How to Plant God's Love in the Garden of Your Heart

Lots of people claim they want God's love in their lives, but what they mean is that they want God to love them—not that they want to love God or others. Love requires sacrifice, and while they are willing to accept God's sacrifice for them, they don't want to be inconvenienced in any manner in return.

But unless we love God and others, we cannot please Him.

Here's how to get started: Break up the soil.

Planting God's love requires a deep-spaded examination of the condition of our hearts. It demands that we thoroughly examine our lives by allowing the Holy Spirit to dig up any sin-hardened clods of selfishness; we have to let the Gardener grub out any rocks of unforgiveness. Love requires an act of our volition, a decision to be willing to give and forgive.

Are you willing to give of yourself to be used by God in the lives of others? Are you willing to forgive those who have hurt you in the past and will hurt you in the future?

Jesus used a parable to describe the conditions found in human hearts. His story explains why some love more easily, while others have a harder time. Why not apply His parable to your own life? Examine your heart for the following conditions:

- *Stony soil:* Some individuals will hear Christ's message of love and accept it gladly. But when it comes time for sacrifice or endurance—and these times come for everyone—the new growth of faith withers. These people have shallow commitments. Love cannot be fruitful without a deep-rooted commitment.

- *Thorny soil:* The most deceptive of all "heart soil" is that which carries the seeds of selfishness, busyness, and distractions. People like this want to respond to Christ's message of love—and they do for a short time—until dormant weeds of self-ishness sprout, take root, and choke out their commitment to love.

- *Good soil:* People with hearts full of good soil have counted the cost, and they are dedicated to making the sacrifices love requires. They are watchful lest other things take the place of real love, and they are careful to let nothing that does not yield true love take root in their hearts.

Paul speaks of love as the "the most excellent way" (1 Corinthians 12:31 NIV) among all other spiritual gifts. This love is supernaturally given to us by the Holy Spirit when we ask Christ to live within us. As Christ's Spirit dwells within us, He inspires us to love as He loved.

However, even though love is the gift of God's Spirit, we are also commanded to love, implying that we can control our loving actions and attitudes by our own will. God puts the gift of His love in our hearts—but we are the ones who must choose to cultivate our ability to demonstrate that love. As we yield ourselves more and more to God, love will grow and bear fruit.

Signs That Grafts to the True Vine Are Healthy

How We Treat Our Neighbors

- We love them as ourselves (Leviticus 19:18).
- We forgive our neighbors' faults and do not repeat gossip (Proverbs 17:9).
- We love as Christ loved (John 15:12), walking in love, giving ourselves as living sacrifices (Ephesians 5:2).
- We regard our brother and sisters in Christ as family, and we treat them affectionately (Romans 12:10).
- We prefer that others be honored rather than ourselves (Romans 12:10).
- We do not participate in anything that would hurt those around us in any way (Romans 13:10).

How We Treat Our Enemies

- We pray for those who mistreat us (Luke 6:28).
- We love our enemies. We do good to those who hate us. We bless those who curse us (Luke 6:27–28).

- We loan to them without expecting repayment (Luke 6: 34-35).
- Our love covers over all wrongs (Proverbs 10:12).

How We Behave Toward Every Person

- We go the extra mile (Matthew 5:41).
- We give to anyone who asks us for anything, and we never turn anyone away (Matthew 5:42).
- We give water to the thirsty (Matthew 10:42), food to the hungry, clothing to the naked, shelter to the traveler, and company to the confined (Matthew 25:35–36).
- We do unto others as we would have done unto us (Luke 6:31).
- We show mercy (Luke 10:37).
- We love without pretense. (Romans 12:9).
- We keep current with our obligations (Romans 13:8).
- We don't commit adultery, kill, steal, lie, or covet others' possessions or relationships (Romans 13:9).
- We forbear and forgive (Colossians 3:13).
- By our lives, we encourage others to love (Hebrews 10:24).

A HARVEST OF LOVE

Roots Planted in Stone

And this is love:
that we walk in obedience to His commands.
As you have heard from the beginning,
his command is that you walk in love.
2 JOHN 6 NIV

Originally there were Ten Commandments on two tablets of stone. In Christ, they were summed up in four words and written on the fleshy tablets of the heart: Love God. Love others.

Distinguishing Tender Sprouts of Love from Self-Deception

Love is not only giving $20 to the community fund drive; it is compassion and forgiveness for the paperboy when he misses the porch, or to the checkout girl when she makes an error, or to the other driver when he cuts you off.

Love is positive action on behalf of another—with possible cost to the lover.

The opposite of love is not hate; the opposite of love is indifference.

We excuse our lack of love with comments like these: "He's so mean!" "She's so nasty!" But the second greatest commandment is that we should love others as we do ourselves. Therefore we should give to others and demand from others no more or no less than what we ask of ourselves and for ourselves.

Some Romeos offer sweet-smelling flowers to their Juliettes as a token of love; God offered us the fragrance of Christ.

Live a life of love,
just as Christ loved us
and gave Himself up for us
as a fragrant offering
and sacrifice to God.

EPHESIANS 5:2 NIV

A HARVEST OF LOVE

Love is the law in Christ's kingdom, the rule of the road on the route to heaven, the assignment in His school, the test of the successful, the coat of arms of His family.

Earnestly seek to love. Make it your life's quest.

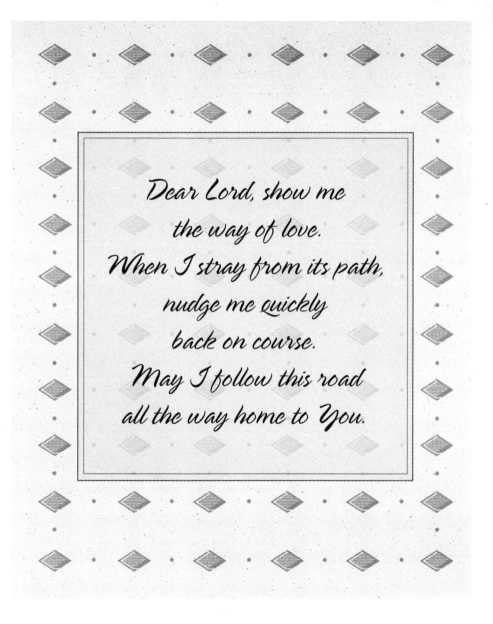

Dear Lord, show me
the way of love.
When I stray from its path,
nudge me quickly
back on course.
May I follow this road
all the way home to You.

Chapter 2

Patient Love
Planting Seeds of Patience

The acts of the sinful nature are obvious:
. . .hatred, discord, jealousy,
fits of rage, selfish ambition.

GALATIANS 5:19–20 NIV

But the fruit of the Spirit is love.

GALATIANS 5:22 NIV

Love is patient.

1 CORINTHIANS 13:4 NIV

Charity suffereth long.

1 CORINTHIANS 13:4

Fertilize Your Brain
A Definition of Patience

The Greek word used in the New Testament for patience —*makrothumein*—is always used to describe forbearance with people, not toleration with circumstances. Biblical patience describes a person who has been wronged and who could easily exact revenge, but who will not do so because of love.

Loving patience does not merely mean waiting out the problem. Rather it means a careful study to maximize its potential for the loved one and the kingdom of God.

Do not mistake tolerance with patient love. Tolerance implies passivity; patient love is active. Toleration is the behavior of a tired old dog that allows the baby to climb all over it and pull its ears. Patience describes the scientist who repeatedly experiments until she achieves the desired beneficial results.

- Loving patience is the parent who persistently disciplines an unruly child in hopes of rearing a godly citizen.
- Loving patience is the spouse who repeatedly confronts a wayward mate with the goal of maintaining their home and marriage.
- Loving patience is the employee who makes an all-out effort to meet an employer's demands as an example of Christian witness and a display of good character.
- Loving patience is a teacher who consistently strives to inspire the student to learn, regardless of the student's aptitude or attitude.
- Loving patience is the pastor who continues to encourage and exhort his congregation in the face of indifference and disbelief, always working to heal and multiply the flock.
- Loving patience is God gently, firmly, and consistently urging us toward Christlike behavior so that Christ's sacrifice will not be in vain. . .so that we are not lost. . .so that we can live eternally with Him.

Bear with each other
and forgive whatever grievances
you may have
against one another.
Forgive as the Lord
forgave you.
And over all these virtues
put on love.

COLOSSIANS 3:13–14 NIV

Many of us can be patient for only a little while. Remember: God forgives us in the same measure we forgive others. So when you're about to lose patience, try a different approach: Instead of counting to ten, ask yourself, "How long do I want God to be patient with me before He sends judgment?"

Rooting Out Impatience
with Understanding
A Mother-in-Law's Gift

Mindy never met her mother-in-law, but if she had not passed away before Mindy and Don married, Mindy thinks they probably would have been good friends.

"From what I hear about my mother-in-law Mary, she was a wonderful, godly woman—warm and generous. And from what Don has told me over and over and over and over again, the world's greatest cook," said Mindy.

But Don's memories of his mother's meals were hard for Mindy to swallow.

"I just can't compete with a ghost," said Mindy. "As far as Don is concerned, his mother was the patron saint of the kitchen! He remembers these wonderful meals she made with homemade bread so light you had to hold it down to take a bite, fresh butter, two kinds of pie. . . And according to Don, she had a recipe for ham and beans that made the angels sing."

When they were first married, Mindy tried to re-create Mary's memorable meals. "I didn't know how to cook at all, so I borrowed Mary's recipe books and studied them. I knew my limitations, so I started small and learned to make a few simple dishes."

As she gained confidence, she tried some food on a grander

scale. "I'll never forget how upset I was when I worked for hours making this big meal for Don using his mother's recipes —and while he ate he rhapsodized about his mother's cooking and never said a word about mine! For a while after that, I quit cooking all together. I had to pray for forgiveness because I resented both Don and his mother."

While necessity is said to be the mother of invention, Mindy said that it is also the mother-in-law of casseroles. "Sooner or later, I realized that we couldn't live on baloney sandwiches forever. I had learned quite a bit from studying Mary's cookbooks, so I started stirring up my own recipes— mostly casseroles at first.

"I would pray about the meals—and my attitude—as I was cooking, and one day the Lord gave me insight into the situation: Don's mother died when he was young; almost his only memories of her were her meals. He wasn't trying to tear me down. He just was missing his mother, and on some level, he was complimenting me by comparing me to her. His loyalty to her kept my meals from being as good in his eyes as hers were.

"I've learned to be patient now with Don's comments about his mother's cooking. In fact, when people compliment my cooking, I tell them, 'My mother-in-law taught me to cook.' And that's true, too. I learned by trying to be as good as her memory."

A HARVEST OF LOVE

Loving patience is acquired only through testing both love and patience. The acquisition may not be pleasant—but it is profitable.

*Patience is
the necessary ingredient
of genius.*

DISRAELI

*Recipe for
Loving Patience*

- Begin with one large vexation and several small irritations well marbled with interruptions and inconveniences.
- Allow the Sword of the Spirit to slice off pride, judgmental attitudes, and self-importance.

- Rub well with the love of Christ and allow to marinate until tender.
- Add a cup each of gentleness, calmness, and understanding with a large dash of self-control.
- Serve with a dollop of perseverance.
- Memorize James 1:3–4, 19.

Knowing this, that the trying of your faith worketh patience.
But let patience have her perfect work,
that ye may be perfect and entire, wanting nothing.
Wherefore, my beloved brethren,
let every man be swift to hear,
slow to speak, slow to wrath.

JAMES 1:3–4, 19

Loving patience is
not a sign of weakness,
but of strength.

Growing in Patience—
Important Notes to Remember

When you are tempted to give up on someone, remember:

And let us not be weary in well doing:
for in due season we shall reap, if we faint not.
GALATIANS 6:9

When you are ready to "blow your stack" at someone, remember:

Be not hasty in thy spirit to be angry:
for anger resteth in the bosom of fools.
ECCLESIASTES 7:9

When settling a dispute with others, remember:

Everyone should be quick to listen,
slow to speak and slow to become angry.
JAMES 1:19 NIV

Leafing Out in Love
A Prayer for Loving Patience

Dear Lord,
I will rest in You and wait patiently for You to answer
my prayers, rather than demand my own way. Let me
not fret myself because of evildoers but react with loving
patience. Let me not be wrathful and stir up strife, but let
me be slow to anger.

Patience in Bloom

When Tom was around, people had to grit their teeth to keep from snarling at him. He was remarkably boneheaded, always cocksure that he knew what he was doing when most of the time he didn't have the faintest idea. On top of that, he insisted that everything had to be done his way. People had to search hard to find even one redeeming quality about him.

He was such a contrast to his wife. Anne was as sweet and considerate as Tom was brash and arrogant. Occasionally, people would ask her how she could tolerate Tom's antics.

"I love him," Anne would answer, "so I guess that's why

I think he's wonderful. It always surprises me that other people can't see his good qualities. I guess I see him with the eyes of love."

When the angels see all that the evil humans do and they question God as to why He tolerates us, His answer must be the same: "I see them with the eyes of love."

God could swat the entire population of the world into oblivion without raising a sweat—and with all the sin and rebellion against Him, it is a mystery why He doesn't. His patient love is the only explanation.

The Sweet Fruit of Patience

If my third grade teacher were teaching today, she probably would end up in jail. Long ago, she had run out of patience with children. Her discipline measures were the subject of many a small child's nightmares.

I was a good student and anxious to please, but numbers were something of a mystery to me—especially multiplication. Whenever I—or any student—got an assigned problem wrong, we would have to stand beside Teacher's desk to correct it while she watched. If we made a mistake, she would crack us on the head with the flat of her hand. Needless to say, we were all terrified.

My fear of numbers remained for almost forty years. I actually avoided some business opportunities because tax forms and accounting were such horrors to me. My fear was especially bad once a month when I had to write checks for household expenses. Some women have PMS: I had PBS—Pre-Bill Syndrome, where I was chased through my dreams by dollar signs and decimal points. Anxiety attacks would plague me a week before I sat down and wrote the checks. And then my hands would actually shake so badly that sometimes my signature was illegible.

Embarrassed, I mentioned my fears to no one, not even my husband. But I prayed a lot about them. Over time, the Lord showed me that He invented numbers to be helpful, not hurtful. They were meant to be my servants, not my master. When He told Adam and Eve to subdue their world, He also meant arithmetic; therefore, I was in charge of numbers and not vice versa. I was to use numbers—not be abused by them.

It took decades to erase the effects of one year of grade school, but God was patient. As long as I needed help with my fear, His perfect love was there to cast it out. And He didn't hit me on the head even once to teach me!

Loving Patience Grows on Rocky Soil

Jake and Jean had been married for five good years—and about twenty-five bad ones. It wasn't that they didn't love each other anymore; they just didn't see eye-to-eye on much of anything. Added to that, each felt obligated to convince the other of his or her position. The result was an almost constant debate that often grew heated. Their friends and children tolerated it the best they could, but sometimes it was tough because Jake and Jean insisted that others take sides in their battles. However discomforting it was for others, they seemed to enjoy the conflict.

Their war of words came to an unexpected and abrupt silence one morning. With the car packed for vacation, Jake and Jean stopped at the local hospital at 9 A.M. Jean was to have a simple, routine test on her esophagus. Then they planned to be on their way by 11:00.

Instead, something went terribly wrong: Jean's esophagus was ripped during the test. When she was given a carbonated soft drink, her chest cavity flooded, and stomach acid began to digest her heart, liver, lungs, and the chest lining. She was literally being eaten alive from the inside out.

At first, the hospital personnel refused to believe that there was anything wrong, but her screams of agony finally convinced them to x-ray her chest. Then the tear was discovered. It would require extensive surgery to repair the tear and the damage to her internal organs. No one knew if she would survive.

After the surgery, with Jean totally sedated for many days, Jake sat beside her bed and held her hand. Later, when she regained painful consciousness, he stayed, too, only leaving to grab a quick bite of food or a shower. He made sure that he was there at every mealtime to feed her meager meals of gelatin and sips of tea.

Because Jean was unable to speak above a hoarse, painful whisper, their bantering ceased. From long years of heated discussion, they knew each other's likes and dislikes so well that Jean could communicate with her eyes and facial expressions. Holding hands through the maze of tubes and monitors, an unspoken but concrete commitment filled the long hours of silence between them more eloquently than any romantic words could ever express.

Because Jean's recovery was impeded by constant mistakes by hospital personnel, Jake transferred her to another hospital in a faraway city, where she received better care. With Jean still helpless and confined in the intensive care unit, Jake sat in the waiting room waiting for his ten-minute visit every hour. At night, he slept in his van in the hospital parking garage in case Jean needed him.

In the end, Jean did not recover, but I know she must have died certain of Jake's love. For those who knew Jean and Jake, his faithful devotion was surprising. Who would have guessed that six weeks of silence would tell more about their love than thirty years of marriage?

A HARVEST OF LOVE

Bearing Fruit
A Prayer for Loving Patience

Dear Lord,
Help me to be patient toward all people
(1 Thessalonians 5:14). *I am in need of patience*
so that I may behave in accordance to the code of
conduct that is pleasing to You, that I may be the
recipient of Your promised blessings (Hebrews
10:36).

I know that the trials I face in my life and in my relationships develop patience. Let patience do a perfect work in me that I may be mature and complete in You, rather than immature and weak (James 1:3–4). *Let me be swift to listen to others, but slow to speak and slow to anger* (James 1:19). *Help me as Your child, chosen by You, to have a heart of mercy, kindness, humility, meekness, and longsuffering. Help me to forgive those who want to pick a quarrel with me—and may I never forget that Christ has forgiven me* (Colossians 3:12–13).

Chapter 3

Love is Kind
Planting Seeds of Loving-Kindness

Love is kind.

1 CORINTHIANS 13:4

Fertilize Your Brain
A Definition of Kindness

Kindness: sympathy, gentleness, benevolence, compassion, friendliness, or good-heartedness.

Kindness: A Balm For the Soul— and Stomach!

"At forty-three years old," said Marilyn, "I unexpectedly found myself not only pregnant but tempest-tossed with severe morning sickness. Frankly, I was a little embarrassed about this ill-timed midlife pregnancy, and we tried to keep it secret while my husband and I adjusted to it ourselves. The secret was a hard one to keep, though, as I was teaching a Sunday school class of my peers—and looking green as grass, I had to occasionally bolt for the powder room!"

Marilyn said that one of the younger women in her class deduced her secret. "Her husband was chronically unemployed, yet she continued to have children. I often suspected that some of them arrived at moments that were not opportune." This young woman telephoned Marilyn early one weekday morning just as the ocean waves of nausea were rising.

"She asked if she could stop in for a moment. I really didn't want to see anybody just then, but she was insistent so I reluctantly agreed. She arrived just about 'high tide.'

"Thankfully, she didn't ask me any questions—but she did bring a beautifully decorated tea basket filled with assorted de-caffeinated herbal flavors, a keepsake mug, honey, and crackers. Her only comment: 'I just wanted to thank you for teaching our class. I learned to enjoy herb teas when I was pregnant. They seemed to settle my stomach.'

"She didn't pry; she just wanted to help. I've never forgotten her loving-kindness."

Sprouting Kindness in Action

Kind, thoughtful acts for a sick friend take only a few moments and a little thought to prepare, but they are fun things to do. Chances are, you'll get much more of a blessing than you give!

Here are some idea starters:

For a man

- a magazine or joke book
- aftershave or cologne
- inexpensive binoculars
- a CD
- cookies, candy, and/or fruit
- a comedy or old-time action video
- novelty socks
- a miniature basketball hoop and mini foam basketball
- a collection of Bible verses

- a deck of cards
- a goldfish and bowl
- homemade soup and/or bread
- a puzzle book
- a little bell to summon help (His caregiver will hate the bell, but he'll love it!)

For a woman

- pretty notes, a pen, and postage stamps
- cologne and/or hand lotion
- scented soap and/or candle
- bath salts
- fancy sweets
- a gift book
- potpourri and/or sachets
- a teacup and saucer
- herbal teas and honey
- a CD
- a comedy or romantic love story on video
- a diary or blank book
- an interesting plant
- a small figurine
- books on tape
- a fancy pillowcase

A HARVEST OF LOVE

For children

- ◆ small toys (There's a huge selection here!)
- ◆ a goldfish and bowl
- ◆ animal crackers
- ◆ books and/or puzzles
- ◆ stuffed animals
- ◆ children's video
- ◆ tapes of children's music or stories
- ◆ drawing supplies

A Rare, Fragrant Variety of Kindness— A Symphony of Love

I have some special friends in an Indiana Amish community, and not long ago their twelve-year-old son developed a brain tumor. The family and medical community did everything they could to heal it, but everyone recognized early on that his condition was hopeless. In the mornings on my way to work, I would drive by their home, located far out in the country, to see if they needed anything.

On a Tuesday morning in late fall, one of the children was standing beside the mailbox waiting for me. She flagged me down and said matter-of-factly, "If you want to see Daniel alive, you should come in. We think he's going to die today."

I pulled my vehicle off the road and entered their humble little house. I could barely recognize the boy; the steroids used to control the tumor had caused his face and body to swell.

I petted his hair and cheeks, but he was already so far gone he could not hear my voice or know my touch. His pupils were contracted, his hands icy; all the signs of imminent death were around him.

A few hours later, I heard that he was gone.

I waited until late afternoon to again stop by the house. The undertaker had claimed the body, and most of the furniture had been cleared out of the house in preparation for the funeral, which would be held in the home the next day.

A row of chairs lined the walls, and the family, mute with sorrow, sat on them to receive guests. All around them, the house was a hive of activity. A man was repairing the kitchen doorjamb with hammer and nails. A group of bearded men was banging away on the roof of the barn. Another group was noisily fixing a dry-rotted spot on the porch. The hammering was almost deafening and certainly distracting. Buggies and cars kept pulling up and the passengers would unload to silently and solemnly shake the hands of the family. There was no point in talking; nothing could have been heard above the racket.

Suddenly, all the hammering ceased.

The hearse pulled up with young Daniel's body on a stretcher. The undertaker whispered a question to one of the young men, and the young man nodded. From the barn, a simple pine coffin was brought into the house. At the sight of it, the family burst into grief-stricken sobbing.

When I saw it, suddenly I knew. All of the repair work around the farm had been done for a single purpose. The work could have been done anytime; it didn't have to be now. But the noisy hammering was actually a symphony of loving-kindness, for it covered up the heartrending sounds parents never wish to hear—that of a small coffin being hammered together for their child.

Kindness comes in all sorts of shapes. The specific shape of the container matters far less than the love it holds.

Showers of Blessings
Start a "Cold Water" Ministry

This is a simple, inexpensive gift, but oh-so-appreciated when someone is thirsty. And giving a simple cup of water comes with the promise of heavenly dividends:

Whosoever shall give to drink
unto one of these little ones
a cup of cold water
only in the name of a disciple,
verily I say unto you,
he shall in no wise lose his reward.

MATTHEW 10:42

I was thirsty,
and ye gave me drink. . . .
Insomuch as ye have done it unto one of
the least of these my brethren,
ye have done it unto me.
MATTHEW 25:35, 40

A HARVEST OF LOVE

- Take a cup of a cold beverage to your neighbor when he/she is doing yard work.

- Set up a water station for runners, walkers, or bikers during fund-raising or marathon events. You can also distribute a brief note bearing a refreshing Bible verse with your phone number or that of your church. People will try to pay you (they will think it is some sort of a fund-raiser and they may also feel strange accepting a free gift), but always refuse any money by saying, "No, it's free—like the love of Jesus."

- Provide a water stop at a local street fair. Again, hand out little cards with information on them. They might read: *A cup of cold water for you, in Jesus' name, courtesy of Your Name or Organization. Contact us at XXX-XXXX if we can be of help.* Keep the literature at a minimum so they can hold on to it for future reference. If you overload people with information at a street fair, much of it will become landfill. Be prepared to hear people's problems on the spot.

- A variation of cold-water ministries is to hand out free hot coffee and chocolate with an information card during outdoor winter activities.

Holy Spirit,
thank You for giving me
Your loving-kindness.

Hidden Blooms of Gold—A Kind Secret

The mystery began on a Monday morning when I found an empty bank bag in the locked drawer of the Sunday school desk. Puzzled, I scratched my head and wondered if I was losing my mind. I knew I had put the entire children's Sunday school collection in that bag and locked it in the drawer. Why wasn't it in there now?

I knew the lock on the drawer hadn't come from Fort Knox, but it seemed secure enough. I checked the drawer for pry marks, but there weren't any. Somehow, someone must have picked the lock and taken the money. I felt sick. What kind of person would take a children's offering of pennies, dimes, and quarters?

I informed the Sunday school superintendent and the pastor. They, too, shook their heads in dismay.

Then I had a suspicion. A boy in the congregation had been into all kinds of trouble. He had a job at the police station on Sunday afternoons, but because his parents lived far out in the country, they left him at the church until it was time for him to go to work. Now, money was missing.

I didn't want to directly accuse him, but he seemed a likely culprit. I pulled him and his parents aside, told them what had happened, and suggested that perhaps the boy shouldn't be in the church alone until the thief was caught. They agreed.

Naïvely confident that the problem was solved, I locked the offering in the desk the following Sunday. Monday, it was gone.

Now began a cat-and-mouse game that lasted almost five years. For months, the money would be where it was supposed to be. Then suddenly there would be a rash of burglaries. It was maddening. We discussed the problem in staff meetings, but since it was only a matter of $4 or $5 each time, no one was motivated to take much action.

After a time, the thefts simply stopped. In fact, they totally slipped my mind until one day a middle-aged woman pulled me aside and shamefacedly handed me a check made out to the Sunday school. As I stared blankly at the check, she gave me a drawer key.

"Can we just keep this between the two of us?" she asked anxiously. "It's important because Mother's reputation is at stake." Then she told me the story.

"When I put Mother in the nursing home, I began to go through her personal effects. I found a bunch of carefully made out deposit slips listing small quantities of change. I wondered about them. Then one day I found a pile of change. After a lot of counting, I realized the amount of change matched the total amounts on the deposit slips. When I asked Mother about it, she said it was the Sunday school offering. That used to be her job, you know—she was the Sunday school treasurer for nearly fifty years. So every now and then, she must have thought of the Sunday school offering and thought she had forgotten to pick it up—so she must have slipped over to collect it. She was holding the money until she could get to the bank to deposit it—but she hasn't driven for ten years!"

I took the check and the key and assured the woman that her secret was safe with me. My heart pricked me, and I wished I had been kinder to the child whom I had suspected of thievery so long ago. At the same time, I couldn't help but be impressed with the kindness and respect this woman was showing her mother. Some caretaker children would have made fun of their parent's eroding mental capacity. Some would have told the story far and wide, laughing at their parent's foolishness. This daughter's kindness demonstrated that she truly understood how to honor her mother.

Sowing Kind Deeds

Here are some concrete ways to sow kindness:

- *Write a thank-you note.* The rule of thumb is if a person has done something for you that took more than fifteen minutes, you should send a thank-you note.

- *Send a single flower.* When someone is having a difficult day, leave a flower with a note telling him or her that you are praying for his or her need. Use your head here. Don't leave a flower for a member of the opposite sex who might misconstrue the meaning.

- *Give a chocolate "kiss."* Same as above—but have a heart and leave a flower if the person is dieting!

- *Run errands.* Is your friend having a busy week? Offer to get the groceries, wash the car, pick up the dry cleaning, etc.

- *Drop off a meal.* For someone time-crunched, with sickness in the house, moving, or blessed with unexpected company, stir together your best quick-fix recipe and drop it off. (I buy cheap casserole dishes at garage sales, so I don't have to worry about them being returned.) Think chili soup; macaroni and cheese; enchiladas; tuna casserole; chicken, broccoli, rice, and cheese casserole; barbecue beef; sloppy joes; noodle soup; etc.

- *Drop off a single-serving meal for someone who lives alone.* When you fix your own meals, cook a little extra. Maybe brown up an additional chop or chicken breast, a few more potatoes, and vegetables. Place the food in compartmentalized paper plates (use two on the bottom to prevent leaks), cover with plastic wrap, and then aluminum foil to transport and store in either the refrigerator or freezer. Single-serving desserts or salads should be wrapped separately.

- *Send care packages to college kids.* Send fast-food coupons and gift certificates, packages of instant coffee, microwave popcorn, insulated coffee mugs, new socks, homemade cookies, highlighters, pens and pencils, or computer disk labels, along with an encouraging note.

Leaves of Kindness

Jenny was in the beginning of her fourth year of college, living in an off-campus apartment, and her finances were tight. She had been waiting tables at a steak house where the patrons normally tipped pretty well, but lately the business had dried up.

"I was having a hard time making ends meet," said Jenny. "I'd cut all the corners I could and worked all the hours they'd give me, but it was still nip and tuck."

With books to be bought and classes to pay for, Jenny was past nip and tuck, and into downright hungry when she saw the familiar face of one of her aunts.

"Her meal cost $15—and she left a $20 tip. Then she came back later that same weekend and left another $20 tip. She must have known that I really needed it. It was the kindest thing."

And be ye kind
one to another.

EPHESIANS 4:32

Blossoming with Kindness
A Prayer

Dear Lord,
Let me treat the stranger as kindly as if he were a lifelong friend, remembering that by this many have entertained angels without knowing it (Leviticus 19:34; Hebrews 13:2). If I see my sister in need, help me not to hide from her but be helpful (Deuteronomy 22:1). Help me to show kindness to those around me. Remind me not to look down on those who bring trouble upon themselves but instead lend them aid, expecting

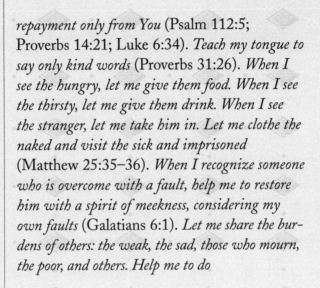

repayment only from You (Psalm 112:5; Proverbs 14:21; Luke 6:34). *Teach my tongue to say only kind words* (Proverbs 31:26). *When I see the hungry, let me give them food. When I see the thirsty, let me give them drink. When I see the stranger, let me take him in. Let me clothe the naked and visit the sick and imprisoned* (Matthew 25:35–36). *When I recognize someone who is overcome with a fault, help me to restore him with a spirit of meekness, considering my own faults* (Galatians 6:1). *Let me share the burdens of others: the weak, the sad, those who mourn, the poor, and others. Help me to do*

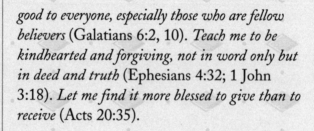

good to everyone, especially those who are fellow believers (Galatians 6:2, 10). *Teach me to be kindhearted and forgiving, not in word only but in deed and truth* (Ephesians 4:32; 1 John 3:18). *Let me find it more blessed to give than to receive* (Acts 20:35).

Chapter 4

Love Does Not Envy
Sowing the Good Seed

The acts of the sinful nature are obvious:
sexual immorality, impurity and debauchery;
idolatry and witchcraft;
hatred, discord, jealousy, fits of rage,
selfish ambition, dissensions, factions and envy;
drunkenness, orgies, and the like.
I warn you, as I did before,
that those who live like this will not inherit
the kingdom of God.
But the fruit of the Spirit is love.
GALATIANS 5:19–22 NIV

Love. . .does not envy.

1 CORINTHIANS 13:4 NIV

Most often, envy grows when we allow selfishness to take root in our hearts. If we are not careful, before long these ugly weeds will choke out the harvest of love that the Spirit longs to reap from our lives.

The Envy That Grows from the Seeds of Selfishness

Marsha and her two sisters were quite young when their mother abandoned them at the front gates of an orphanage. Despite the pain and trauma, Marsha has some fond memories of those days because the orphanage encouraged the sisters to stick together.

"We were so close," Marsha remembers. "None of us ever cried alone. If I or one of my sisters was hurt or lonely, we comforted each other."

Eventually, the girls were farmed out to separate foster homes, but they saw each other at the public school where they all attended.

"I felt like I didn't need any other friends as long as I had my sisters. We sat together at lunch and held hands walking to classes."

However, in her foster home, Marsha didn't feel accepted. "I didn't know how to do things properly. No one had ever taught me simple manners, like chewing with my lips shut, putting my napkin in my lap, or covering a sneeze. I knew I was lacking social graces, but I didn't have a clue as to what they were."

The library provided Marsha with that expertise. "I'd check out books on manners and etiquette, and pretty soon, I knew exactly what to do in any social occasion. Good manners opened all kinds of doors for me. They gave me confidence."

Marsha soon had a larger circle of friends beyond her sisters. She was nominated for homecoming queen and won. But that night was the first time since their mother had left them that Marsha felt rejection from a family member.

"When I was crowned, I remember seeing all these smiling faces and everybody clapping. I was looking around for my sisters. I wanted to see them happy for me. At first, I couldn't find them, and then I caught a glimpse of them as they were leaving the gym. They were angry because I won." Marsha's night was ruined and her sisters wouldn't speak to her for weeks afterward. Her sisters had allowed envy to take the place of the love in their hearts.

Marsha has gone on to write numerous books about manners and has appeared on many national television programs as an etiquette expert. Unfortunately, however, her successes have driven an even deeper wedge between her and her sisters.

"I rarely tell them anything good that is happening to me. If they hear about it, it is secondhand. I've heard many celebrities say that as long as they were struggling to succeed, their families supported them. Once they made it, the only family they had left were shirttail kin wanting to borrow money," said Marsha.

Is our love for others dependent on what we can get from them? Does envy of another's success root out the tender love seedlings sprouting in our hearts? We need to be careful, and open our hearts to the Master Gardener's loving weeding.

Beware of Poison Envy!

There are two slightly different varieties of envy: One covets the possessions of other people; the other begrudges neighbors what they have. The first type is very human; it means simply that we long to have the good things we see others enjoying. Because this is so natural to our selfish hearts, it is hard to avoid. The second variety is more insidious, however, because envy like this does not simply want what the neighbor has; instead, it doesn't want the neighbor to have the prized possession either.

Envy, the Destroyer of Spiritual Fruit

Envy, the triplet sister of covetousness and lust, has ruined many a friendship, marriage, and family. Guard your heart carefully against the first signs of it! It can and will destroy loving relationships quicker than nearly anything.

Here are some biblical examples of relationships eaten up by envy:

- *Cain and Abel.* These two brothers both offered sacrifices to God for their sins. While both understood that a blood sacrifice was required, Cain offered vegetables instead. Because he saw God was pleased with Abel's sacrifice, Cain complained to God about the cosmic unfairness of it. God told him, "If you do well"—or quit sinning—"you will be blessed, too." God's blessing on Abel galled Cain so much that he killed his brother. (Genesis 4:4–8)

- *Sarah and Hagar.* Although God had promised to give Abraham and Sarah children, Sarah decided that she would take matters into her own hands. In keeping with the custom of the day, she encouraged Abraham to have children with her servant Hagar. Abraham didn't appear to have any objections, the plan succeeded, and Ishmael was born. But the plan backfired in Sarah's face, and she was so consumed with envy that she banished Hagar and her son into the desert. They would have died there if an angel of the Lord had not intervened. (Genesis 16:5–6; 21:9–10)

- *Joseph and his brothers.* Jacob, whose name was changed to Israel, favored his son Joseph over his older brothers. No doubt demonstrated in many ways, this favoritism especially chafed the brothers when Israel gave Joseph a coat of many colors —the costume of a king or ruler. Joseph didn't help matters when he apparently bragged about his favored position by relating dreams that emphasized his exalted status. When Israel sent Joseph to check up on his older brothers' work, their envy was so strong, they seized the opportunity to sell him to some Ishmaelites and deceived Israel by implying that Joseph was eaten by wild animals. Israel's profound grief made the brothers regret their actions. (Genesis 37:3–11, 19–20)

- *Saul and David.* Totally loyal to King Saul, David performed great acts of bravery and bailed Saul out of a potentially disastrous defeat at the hands of the Philistine army. Barely more than a boy, David captured the imagination of the Israelite nation, who jubilantly sang his praises. Saul expressed his gratitude toward David by repeatedly trying to have him killed. Eventually, his preoccupation with destroying David divided his family and cost him his kingship and life. (1 Samuel 18:8–9, 29)

- *Miriam, Aaron, and Moses.* Envious of their younger brother's success, Miriam and Aaron criticized Moses' mixed-race marriage, implying that they would be better leaders than their brother. As a result, God struck Miriam with leprosy. While Aaron cried out to God for her healing, only Moses' prayer healed her. (Numbers 12:1–14)

- *The Jewish religious leader and Jesus.* The chief priests and elders had lost credibility due to Jesus' powerful ministry and popularity. Filled with envy, they incited a crowd to call for Jesus' crucifixion. Shortly after Jesus' crucifixion, resurrection, and ascension, the Jewish temple was destroyed along with the system of priests. (Matthew 27:18; Mark 15:10; John 11:47–48)

Stamp Out the Blight of Envy with Faith

Although Marcy had a tough time as a real estate broker in a town dominated by a pervasive "good old boys" network, she had worked hard to make her agency the busiest in the entire city. Most of her agents were housewives looking for flexible scheduling so they could care for their families and still generate a good income. Marcy understood the pressures of working and rearing a family, and she made a special effort to be flexible with her agents. As a dedicated Christian businesswoman, she often helped out her employees financially and in other ways, too. She didn't count them as merely employees, but as friends. If they needed something—in business or personally —she tried to meet that need.

As the agency grew, Marcy became aware that some of her

employees were envious of her success. "What they didn't understand was that I had taken all the financial risks and bought the agency. They didn't have expenditures to keep the doors open, the lights on, and the equipment running. They seemed to think I shouldn't make any money because my husband had a good job, that I should support their efforts for free," said Marcy.

While she tried to explain that she was paying the highest percentages per sale in town and that she had additional expenses and risks, some of the agents refused to understand. However, Marcy never expected them to try to cheat her.

Shortly before Christmas, Marcy was surprised to discover that three of her best and most experienced agents were leaving her to work for another agency. "They didn't even give me a chance to meet the offer of the other agency. It was a done deal," said Marcy.

"When they told me they were leaving, it was like I wasn't even in the room. But I had a complete peace. It was like God said to me, 'I've always been good to you. Whatever they do, it's not going to touch you.' "

Marcy put the entire situation in God's hands. And then on the practical, real-life level, she got busy.

In investigating the departing agents' listings, Marcy discovered that all of their listings were set to expire on their last day of work. They planned to take all of the renewal listings to their new agency. Marcy got on the phone and called the listings. All of the best accounts agreed to stay with Marcy.

"Personally, I'm hurt," Marcy admitted. "And I'm afraid that they aren't going to find things quite as rosy as they thought. But I know God will always be my shield."

When the blight of others' envy attacks our gardens, we too can rely on God.

Grudge not
one against another,
brethren,
lest ye be condemned:
behold, the judge
standeth before the door.

JAMES 5:9

A HARVEST OF LOVE

Do You Have Poison Envy?

Envy is more of a problem for some people than it is for others. Some people are jealous of their mates' time or their work companions' promotions. Others are envious of their own children's success. Some resent their in-laws. Other people find themselves jealous when a friend appears to prefer another's company. But too much love never causes a mate or a friend to be jealous: Only selfishness causes jealousy and envy.

Envy is toxic both to our souls and to our ability to love. It stands in the way of love because it demands, "Me! Me! Me!" as the focus of attention. It chills the hearts of our loved ones by casting our own greedy shadows over them. And envy not only hurts our loved ones and us; it is displeasing to God. Listed as one of the works of the flesh in Galatians 5, envy is symptomatic of an unrepentant soul—a soul in danger.

Remember, loving our neighbor as ourselves means we rejoice in their blessings as much we would rejoice in our own.

Envy Checklist

- Do you envy other people's success? Wealth? Position?
- Do you envy other people's happiness? Mate? Family? Children?
- Do you envy other people's physical appearance?

- Do you envy other people's talents? Charisma? Spiritual gifts?
- Do you envy other people's material possessions? Home? Car? Vacation? Inheritance?
- Do you envy other people's health? Age?

Rooting Out Envy
So Love Can Grow
A Prayer

Holy Spirit,
I confess my envy and I renounce it. I ask You to
fill me with Your Spirit so that I will not live in
envy according to the flesh, but in love according
to Your Spirit.

With Your help, I will not fret because of
evildoers or be envious against those who

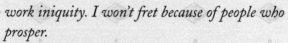

work iniquity. I won't fret because of people who prosper.

I will live honestly, not in strife or in envy. I will lay aside all malice and all guile and hypocrisies and envies and all evil speaking.

By abiding in You, I will love without envy (Galatians 5:25; Psalm 37:1, 7; Romans 13:13; 1 Peter 2:1).

Chapter 5

Love Does Not Boast
Seeds of Loving Humility

Charity. . .vaunteth not itself.

1 CORINTHIANS 13:4

The acts of the sinful nature are obvious:
. . .jealousy. . .selfish ambition. . .envy;
. . .those who live like this will not
inherit the kingdom of God.
But the fruit of the Spirit is love.
GALATIANS 5:20–22 NIV

Love. . .
does not boast.

1 CORINTHIANS 13:4 NIV

We often make ourselves feel better about our accomplishments —or lack thereof—at the expense of others. But true love says, "Look at wonderful you!"—not, "Look at wonderful me!"

Like clouds. . .without rain is a man who boasts.

PROVERBS 25:14 NIV

Toxic Vines, Deadly Fruit— Some Subtle Signs of Pride

Most of us recognize the "Hey, baby! I'm the best thing this side of sliced bread" type of boasting, but many show-off behaviors and windbag speeches go unnoticed—usually by the perpetrator! Check the following list of unloving, bragging statements and actions. See if they remind you of anyone you know (like yourself).

- Controls the conversation by focusing all the attention on self.

- Never listens to anyone else.

- Interrupts others to interject own opinions.

- Informs others of prowess in financial matters, sports, business, sexual affairs, and so on.

- Dwells on offenses against self and retaliates.

- Never, never, never forgives.

- Never admits any personal flaws or shortcomings. Never says, "I'm sorry," "I was wrong," or "Forgive me."

- Openly challenges and undermines anyone in authority. Must be in control.

- Spreads gossip with little or no concern for the harm done to others.

- Looks for a payoff before coming to anyone's aid.

- Looks for self-enhancing relationships. Picks out only rich, powerful, beautiful people as companions and looks for a way to garner perks from the friendships.

- Believes winning is all that counts, but feels justified in pointing out other people's hypocrisies.

- Openly flirts with members of the opposite sex; often blatantly makes a play for sexual favors.

- Enjoys embarrassing others. Likes to insult others but says it is all in fun.

- Berates others, and if they don't fight back, considers that the attack was justified.

- Borrows money with no intention of repaying; spends money irresponsibly; steals and cheats.

- Feels no guilt about anything and has no intention of changing to accommodate anyone.

- Has a short temper and will vent anger in any convenient way—verbally or physically.

- Looks for people who are in a weakened position to taunt or harass.

- Favorite quotes: "I can meet all your needs." "You don't deserve forgiveness." "That's just the way I am. You'll just have to accept it." "He or she needs me."

Authentic love is always more convinced of its own unworthiness than of its own merit.

Tender Vines of Humility— The Eyes of Love

Pride is a particularly vicious sin because it manifests itself in a variety of insidious ways. One of those ways is to dwell on our own merits while failing to recognize the value of others.

When I was a child, my mother insisted that I play with a little girl in our church. Walinda was a homely little thing with terrible body odor, greasy hair, and rotting teeth. She didn't know how to play anything. I didn't want to play with her. I couldn't see past her appearance and odor.

Some years later, all grown-up, my husband and I ran into Walinda at a restaurant. I recognized her instantly. She had not changed a bit: same greasy hair, same snagged teeth, same body odor. But now she was married and had a child.

As I looked at them, feeling the same distaste I had as a child, the Lord nudged me, and I looked closer. When I did, I was amazed by the way Walinda's husband and child looked at her. The man obviously thought she was the most beautiful creature ever to draw breath. And her daughter was equally smitten. Clearly, Walinda was a wonderful wife and mother.

I learned a lesson from Walinda. When I should have asked God for eyes of love, I had been so shallow that I couldn't see past her physical appearance to the soul her husband, child, my mother, and probably everyone else could see. Walinda's exterior may have seemed unattractive—but how little that mattered when her interior was more lovely than that of any beauty queen!

A true lover doesn't seek to glorify herself but instead admires the object of her affection.

Oh, God,
give me eyes of love
that I can see people as
You see them—
and see myself as
You do, too.

Be completely humble and gentle;
be patient, bearing with one another in love.
EPHESIANS 4:2

Remind Me, Lord, Not to Boast
A Prayer for Help

Dear Lord,

Sometimes I'm so busy thinking about the good things about myself that I forget to notice the wonderful qualities of others. All too often I spend my time letting others know—in an oh-so-subtle way—how impressed they should be with my performance and qualities, rambling on and on about my job promotion, my new house, or my career. Forgive me, Lord. Nudge me with Your Spirit whenever You hear me begin to boast.

Chapter 6

Love Is Not Proud
Planting the Seeds of Humble Love

So I say, live by the Spirit,
and you will not gratify the desires of the sinful nature. . . .
The acts of the sinful nature are obvious. . . .
I warn you, as I did before,
that those who live like this
will not inherit the kingdom of God.
GALATIANS 5:16, 19, 21 NIV

Charity. . .
is not puffed up.

1 Corinthians 13:4

Love. . .is not proud.

1 Corinthians 13:4 NIV

Pride is deadly to love. Take note of what pride did to Lucifer's career and relationships and what it will mean to his future.

How art thou fallen from heaven,
O Lucifer, son of the morning!
How art thou cut down to the ground,
which didst weaken the nations!
For thou hast said in thine heart,
"I will ascend into heaven,
I will exalt my throne above the stars of God. . . .
I will be like the most High."
Isaiah 14:12–14

Knowledge puffs up, but love builds up.
1 Corinthians 8:1 NIV

A HARVEST OF LOVE

True love is not too proud to learn from its mistakes. It is happy to be corrected.

A Wild Seed—Pride or Humility?

When the new family up the road from the little church decided to join another assembly in town, the country congregation was stung. Everyone at the church had been friendly to them, the husband explained to the pastor, but they had decided to worship at a church that had indoor plumbing.

When the congregation heard his reason, they sniffed, "Too good for outhouses, huh? Pride is a terrible sin! If outdoor toilets were good enough for the twelve disciples and the apostle Paul, they ought to be good enough for anybody!"

So the little church agreed that indoor toilets were an unnecessary expense and a waste of the Lord's tithe. If people wanted to worship with them, they could use the outhouse or wait until they went home. People shouldn't be coming to church to go to the bathroom anyway!

Proud of their humility, the little country church picked up the welcome mat and slowly died—one person at a time. And what about our lives? Is there an area of "humility" that puffs us up with pride?

Recognizing a Poison Weed

Pride goes before destruction,
a haughty spirit before a fall.
PROVERBS 16:18 NIV

Pride can't. . .
- ◆ say, "I'm sorry."
- ◆ make amends.
- ◆ ask for help.
- ◆ receive help.
- ◆ understand another's hurt.
- ◆ please God.
- ◆ be selfless.
- ◆ be joyful.
- ◆ share feelings or emotions.
- ◆ succeed.

◆

Roots of Humble Love

My husband is a good guy, but he's very fussy about cleanliness in a Felix Unger-sort of a way. And he has a weak stomach.

I didn't know how he would react to the general mess that small children make.

When our first child, a daughter, was born, my husband was totally captivated by her. By the hour, he studied her dainty features, played peek-a-boo and other baby games, gave her baths, and wonder of wonders, changed her diapers! But she had a very sensitive stomach and was subject to projectile vomiting and diarrhea, so she frequently required head-to-toe clothing changes. Me too. Because I was her primary caregiver, I usually bore the brunt of these eruptions.

However, on one of the few occasions when I left the two of them alone, I came home to find Baby plunked in her tub happily splashing away and Hubby covered with strained peas and all matter of body fluids that had leaked out of one end or another from his darling little cherub. As she churned up the bathwater with her little dimpled hands and feet, spattering it all over everything, Hubby looked at me out of the corner of his eye.

"Babies," he said with a touch of exasperation, "are nice, but they sure are grubby!"

Indeed they are. But so is true love. True love lays aside its pride. Like my husband with my daughter, true love allows itself to get messy.

Dangerous Germination—
Deadly Pride

Chicago's Union Station is a fascinating place to watch people. In the space of an hour, you can see everyone from the rich and famous to panhandling beggars. One year before Christmas, with the temperature outside hovering around zero, as I waited there for my train with a cup of coffee, a well-dressed, middle-aged woman with a proud figure asked if she could join me at my small table. She parked her overloaded luggage next to me and asked me to watch her things while she bought some stir-fried vegetables from a nearby vendor.

When she came back, she regally introduced herself, shook my hand, and then to my great surprise, pulled out a fine china plate, a place setting of silver, and a linen napkin. She dumped the contents of the Styrofoam container on the plate, spread the napkin on her lap, and began her repast with impeccable manners; she might have been dining at the Ritz-Carlton rather than a train station.

Over the next half hour, she told me her amazing story. In the midst of it, she casually dropped an important detail: She was homeless.

Less than a decade ago, she had been a private secretary for the president of a Fortune 500 company, she said. When he retired, she had been "retired" too. I was within a half an inch of buying her a train ticket and taking her home with me when she informed me that over the last eight years she just had not been able to find a job that paid as well as her old job had. Oh, she had been offered many jobs, but they wanted to start her out at a smaller wage. She was worth a better salary, she assured me; after all, her skills were still sharp. She simply wasn't going to take less money.

As we talked, she told me about how she survived on the street in the winter. The train station was a good place to get in out of the elements, she informed me, but one needed to dress well or they would find themselves back on the streets. Fruitcake, I was informed, was a key element in the diet of the homeless at this time of year.

"You buy them on sale and they last a long time," she said. "They keep."

As her story unfolded, she revealed that she had two sons on the West Coast who had no idea that she was living on the street. "They would like to come see me, but I've been putting them off until I get back on my feet. I've got several grandchildren that I've never seen, but I'm not going to go visiting until I can go first-class," she said firmly, a glint of fire in her eyes.

When my train was announced, I gently asked her if she would like to have my pocket New Testament.

"Oh, no!" she said, her voice tinged with horror. "I never

ask anybody for help! And that includes God!"

"You don't have to ask Him for help if you don't want to. You might find the stories interesting, though, especially at Christmas. You can read about God's gift to the world and you," I said, thinking that the Holy Spirit had used the story of Christ's birth to crack far tougher nuts.

"Well, if God wants to give me a Christmas present, He can get me a good job! Then we'll talk!" This was obviously her final word on the subject.

As I shook hands with her and took my leave, I mourned for this attractive, intelligent woman who was in such obvious need but was so maimed by pride that she couldn't accept love either from her family or God.

What about you? Is there an area in your life where your pride is blocking the love that God wants to show you?

❖

Turning Over a New Leaf

Betsy and Diane had been friends ever since their children were born. Actually, they were more than friends; they were almost like sisters. Over the years they had traded secrets and baby-sitting, gone shopping, spring-cleaned together, talked over their problems, and confided their hopes and dreams. After they quit having children, both women noticed that they were out of shape, so they began walking and dieting together.

Said Betsy: "Restoring our figures became a big deal for us. Several babies earlier, Diane had had a very pretty shape and I was always so-so, but we both recognized that we were sliding downhill—fast!"

Although both women were happily married to men who were well satisfied with their wives' figures, having a youthful body shape became something of an obsession for them.

"Here's what was so sad: We were so focused on looking good that we neglected what was really important," said Betsy. "I realized one day that I prayed more about losing weight than I did for my children's salvation and their state of mind! What did that say about me as a mother? As a Christian woman? What would it profit me if I had a great figure and my children went to hell? Someday my body was going to rot in the grave anyway, but my children could live in heaven forever!

"I started fasting and praying for my children and put my body and its shape in God's hands. I do some moderate exercises and eat healthy because my body is God's temple and I am responsible for it, but I'm not going to risk my children's eternity because of my pride."

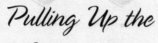

Pulling Up the
Weeds of Pride
A Prayer

Dear Lord,
I know that You hate pride and that it is an
abomination in Your sight (Proverbs 6:16–17).
Forgive me for my pride. I recognize that my
pride is a chain that binds me to corrupt living
and renders me incapable of becoming a truly
loving person (Psalm 73:6). In the name

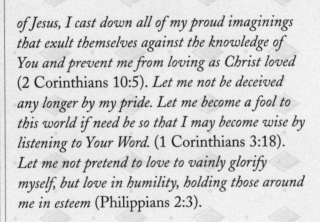

of Jesus, I cast down all of my proud imaginings that exult themselves against the knowledge of You and prevent me from loving as Christ loved (2 Corinthians 10:5). *Let me not be deceived any longer by my pride. Let me become a fool to this world if need be so that I may become wise by listening to Your Word.* (1 Corinthians 3:18). *Let me not pretend to love to vainly glorify myself, but love in humility, holding those around me in esteem* (Philippians 2:3).

Chapter 7

Love Is Not Rude
Planting Seeds of Courteous Love

*Charity. . .
doth not behave itself
unseemly.*

1 CORINTHIANS 13:4–5

When we are rude, we are really just demonstrating our self-ishness, the real nature of our hearts. True love is courteous, gentle, polite, deferring to others.

Love. . .
is not rude.

1 CORINTHIANS 13:4–5 NIV

Digging Deep to Root Out Rudeness

I was in a hurry—a big hurry.

Driving along the four-lane highway leading into Fort Wayne, Indiana, I found myself behind a big old yellow car hogging the left lane. The right, slower lane was jammed with cars placidly tootling along at the speed limit—mostly just below it—enjoying the bright spring sunshine. But this yellow car was puttering along, maddeningly slower than the speed limit, neatly and completely plugging the left passing lane.

I pulled into the left lane behind the yellow car and moved up close behind the rear bumper. The driver paid no attention. I turned on my headlights and flashed the brights off and on. Still no response. The clock on the dash was ticking away the minutes, but the driver of the yellow car showed no hurry, apparently totally oblivious to my growing frustration and time schedule.

While I am normally a patient person, I was quickly becoming irate with this driver. What kind of rude, inconsiderate person would block up all the traffic? Nearly frothing at the mouth and gnawing the steering wheel with frustration, I pulled up next to the car at a stoplight with my window rolled down, ready to give the driver a piece of my mind. To my great shock, a familiar face looked back at me: It was my sister Rose.

"Becky!" she cried with joy.

Instantly, my anger evaporated. Knowing Rose as I do, I knew she meant no harm and that she would never knowingly cause anyone any inconvenience. She was probably driving in the left lane because she supposed that by doing so she was staying out of the way of the other drivers. I knew she didn't have a malicious bone in her body.

I greeted her sheepishly and drove on, glad it was me that pulled up next to her rather than someone else who might have hurt her feelings by doing just what I wanted to do a few seconds earlier.

Out of this experience grew my new driving motto: Love the other driver as you would your sister—even when they're hogging the passing lane.

A HARVEST OF LOVE

Some receive love as though to do so is to offer the other a compliment. But a true lover cannot ever get over the surprise that he is loved.

Some fifty years ago, my father agreed to pastor a congregation in northern Illinois that was in the throes of a division. Because of infighting and conflict, the church had dwindled down to five elderly people—and they weren't getting along either.

The first Sunday Dad occupied the pulpit, one deacon posted a drawing of Satan at the front of the church. "See all of these empty pews?" he demanded of the others. "It is because Satan is sitting in them! We might as well see him so we remember who we're worshipping with!"

The other elder, who was the leader of the opposing faction, told him to take it down. The first deacon refused. So the opposing elder picked him up and threw him against the wall. Dad knew he had his work cut out for him!

Because the church paid almost no salary, Dad worked as an electrician to support the family. The Rural Electrification Act had just been passed, and farmers all over the countryside were getting newfangled electric wiring put in their homes. As Dad ran the wire and put in outlets and lights, he used it as an opportunity to also spread the gospel. Soon, the rickety old church building was so full that people wondered if the floor would support the weight of the crowds from one Sunday to the next.

The question of a new floor came to the church board, which was comprised of the original five elderly people who had since abandoned their grievances to join forces against the tide of newcomers. They firmly and forcefully voted down a new floor.

"Why put in a new floor?" one elder argued. "The growth in this church will not last. These Johnny-come-latelies will more than likely quit coming soon!" He ended his diatribe with some remarks about Dad's presumption for even suggesting a new floor.

Dad was greatly discouraged, but he turned the matter over to the Lord.

That night, the elderly man's even-older mother died. As soon as Dad heard of her death, he knew the elder would be in a bit of a pickle. "He was mad at me and had publicly been insulting. I knew he was going to have a hard time swallowing his pride to ask me to preach his mother's funeral."

Dad made up his mind in advance that he would not make the man squirm, nor would he show any animosity, only God's love.

After the elder called every other preacher in town, all of whom declined to preach the funeral, he hesitantly called Dad and asked him to preach his mother's funeral. Dad, of course, agreed.

Then the man cleared his throat and asked reluctantly, "I know I was against putting in a new floor, but do you think the floor of the church will hold up for Mother's funeral?"

Dad told him that he sure hoped so.

After the funeral, the elder paid out of his own pocket for a new floor to be installed in the church. "In Memory of Mother," read the dedication plaque. And on that planking, the church's congregation grew and grew.

What the plaque should have said was: "Charity doth not behave itself unseemingly."

Bloom With Love—A Loving Manners Test

It's one thing to have company manners, but it's quite another to show courtesy and respect to your family. It's true that they are more or less stuck with you, but if you love them, you'll be on your best behavior around them, too. See how you do on this test.

- ◆ Husbands, when is the last time you opened the car door for your wife? This last week—add 10 points; in the last month—add 5 points; not since your honeymoon—subtract 25 points unless you're a newlywed.

- Wives, when is the last time you got "prettied up" just for your husband? In the last week—add 10 points; in the last month—add 5 points; not since your honeymoon—subtract 25 points unless you're a newlywed.

- Rate your table manners at an average meal: Polished—add 10 points; adequate—0 points; if you talk with your mouth full—subtract 5 points.

- You only bring up subjects of general interest at the table: Always—add 10 points; mostly—add 5 points; you talk continually about yourself or refuse to converse unless you are the subject of the conversation—subtract 10 points.

- Do you start arguments at mealtime? Never—add 10 points; once in a while if it is an election year—add 0 points; often—subtract 5 points; every meal—no points for you! Go to your room until you can behave!

- Do you interrupt people (including children, of course) who are still speaking? Rarely—add 10 points; occasionally—add 5 points; all the time—subtract 5.

Score: 40–50 points: Good job! Keep it up!

30–40 points: Not bad. Brush up a bit and you'll be wonderful to live with.

0–30 points: I'm glad I don't live with you! You can love your family much better with a little effort at courtesy and kindness.

0 and below points: What can I say? Your family has my sympathy.

A Prayer for Help

Remind me, Lord,
that true love is never rude.
Help me to commit myself to
loving courtesy,
all the time,
with everybody.

Chapter 8

Love Is Not Self-Seeking
Planting the Seeds of Selfless Love

Love. . .

is not self-seeking.

1 CORINTHIANS 13:4–5 NIV

Jesus loved us so much that He gave His best:
- ◆ His love.
- ◆ His life.
- ◆ His all.

Some people have never truly loved anyone in their entire lives. They look at every situation and wonder how they can manipulate it to benefit themselves rather than use it for the advantage of another. These people will be eternally lonely if they do not allow God's Spirit to change their hearts.

Jesus said to his disciples,
"If anyone would come after me,
he must deny himself and take up his cross and follow me.
For whoever wants to save his life will lose it,
but whoever loses his life for me will find it.
What good will it be for a man
if he gains the whole world,
yet forfeits his soul?"
MATTHEW 16:24–26

Spontaneous Fruit of Love

It was Christmas Eve, and Grace had her day carefully planned. New to town, she had dreaded spending Christmas away from her parents and siblings, so she carefully planned to fill it to the brim with wonderful people and great activities.

She had a few last-minute preparations to make for tomorrow's dinner, a dish to prepare for tonight's party, presents to wrap, phone calls to make, and then a hair appointment. Sometime this afternoon, her son and daughter would be home from college, and then they would dress for the social event of the season: a grand party at a lovely Victorian mansion hosted by a gracious new friend. After that, the family would attend the midnight candlelight Christmas Eve service.

Tomorrow would be wonderful, too. A charming family would join them for supper. She could hardly wait for her college-age children to meet the children of their new friends. They had similar interests and she just knew that the families would mesh.

Ready to plunge into her busy day, Grace paused to answer the phone. Her daughter's hoarse voice was interrupted by hacking coughs.

"Mama? I'm sick. I can't come home."

She hadn't been able to even keep water down for three days. She had a high fever and chills. There was no way she could manage the six-hour drive home.

"I didn't even think. I did what any parent would do in similar circumstances," said Grace. "I just told her, 'We'll come get you.' I didn't know if she had pneumonia or just a mean ol' flu bug, but it didn't matter, because she needed me and I was going to be there."

Grace spent more than an hour calling everyone to change all her plans. Meanwhile, her husband gassed up the car and was waiting in the driveway with the engine idling.

Said Grace: "We drove twelve hours straight in order to pick her up and get back for Christmas morning. After that, we had a very quiet day. In a way, I felt bad about missing all of the activities and fun, but it was really nothing. We wanted to make sure our twenty-two-year-old baby was cared for."

Real love doesn't count the cost to self.

*If there was
some shortcut to loving,
the Bible would have mentioned it.
But over and over,
we are told to love with
the self-sacrificing yearning
for the best interest of others.*

CARL V. BINKLEY

A HARVEST OF LOVE

Growing Selflessness in Rocky Hearts

Many parents are so selfishly absorbed in themselves that they don't discipline and guide their young ones. Today, lack of parental control is a common problem, but not long ago, too much parental control was just as much of a problem, often with disastrous outcomes. Selfishness was the root cause then as now.

In 1946, it came as a surprise to everyone—including Harry and Edna—that after more than twenty-five years of marriage their first child was on its way.

Early in their marriage, Harry and Edna had wanted children, but they had given up on having them. Disappointed, they spent their lives acquiring considerable wealth and position within their local church, while they amused themselves criticizing the way others brought up their children.

Now, they greeted the possibility of becoming parents with enthusiasm. They would be the most perfect parents who ever lived. Their child would be the perfect child. They would show everyone how a child *should* be reared.

When Joy was born, everyone couldn't help but think how odd the almost-elderly Harry and Edna looked holding the newborn. Joy was tiny and exquisite, perfection in miniature. She had flaxen hair, wide blue eyes, and a lively wit—a little too lively for Harry and Edna, who taught her to be seen but not heard and to only speak when spoken to.

True to their determination to be perfect parents with the perfect child, as Joy grew she was not permitted any television, movies, records, comic books, candy, gum, slacks, jeans, pedal pushers, shorts, or sweatshirts. Her playmates were strictly screened for breeding, refinement, character, and church affiliation. Few made the cut. Joy's clothing and hairstyle harkened back to a style not seen since the repeal of Prohibition.

This was fine when Joy was very young, but by the time she reached sixth grade, her rosebud mouth developed something of a permanent pout. She humbly went along with her parent's wishes, but a storm of rebellion was brewing in Joy's breast.

Upon her graduation with honors from high school, Harry and Edna sent her away to a strict Christian college. On the day she received her diploma from college, she stood in cap and gown and announced to her stunned parents that she never wanted to see or hear from them again.

"You have never loved me. You only looked at me as an accessory for your own lives and pleasure. You've never allowed me any self-expression and have made me into an oddity to suit yourselves. Don't ever contact me again," she told them. And with that, she turned on her heel and walked away.

Amid angry predictions that she would starve without their money, Harry and Edna waited for Joy to return to them. When she did not, they softened a little and sent her letters and cards

A HARVEST OF LOVE

—even money—telling her that if she'd say she was sorry, all would be forgiven. Their letters came back, unopened and marked "Return to Sender" in Joy's own hand. If they called on the telephone, she hung up.

Over the years they heard snatches of her life via the grapevine. Joy had a successful career, married a wealthy man, and gave birth to four children. When Harry lay on his death-bed, Edna sent word to Joy, but she didn't come. Instead, she slipped in the back of the church during his funeral and left while the congregation sang the final hymn. She didn't return home again until Edna died.

Joy was anxious to settle the estate and get back to her life. As she stood before Edna's coffin, looking at her mother's face for the first time in more than ten years, the pastor joined her, thinking perhaps she wanted to talk about her stormy relationship with her parents.

With bitterness, Joy told him: "By the end of my senior year of college, I finally accepted the fact that my parents never would love me unless I was exactly who and what they wanted me to be. I didn't want to be that person. In some ways, I suppose, they were trying to do what they thought was best for me, but they didn't care about me, only about what they wanted."

Thus the tragic, selfish circle was complete: Harry and Edna wouldn't love Joy unless she'd do and be exactly what they wanted. Joy wouldn't love her parents because they weren't exactly who she wanted them to be.

Forget about remaking your loved ones into the people you want them to be. Instead, love them the way they are. If that seems hard, ask God to give you a glimpse of who He made them to be. Discover their uniqueness. Rejoice in their one-of-a-kind gifts to the world. That's the way selfless love works.

Nothing is sweeter than love,
nothing higher,
nothing broader,
nothing better,
either in heaven or earth;
because love is born of God.

THOMAS À KEMPIS

The greatest happiness of life is the conviction that we are loved, loved for ourselves, or rather loved in spite of ourselves.

VICTOR HUGO

A Lifetime Harvest of Selfless Love

I didn't know that Aunt Ruth's diaries existed until shortly before her death. She was in her late nineties by then, and although her health was still fairly good, some inner urge prompted her to began the process of getting rid of her personal effects. She hated to be a nuisance—even if she was going to be dead—and she was tidying up her life.

Born in 1902, she started writing in her diaries as a youngster. Now, my father told me, she was rereading them one at a time and destroying them.

Alarmed, I called her. "Please don't throw away any more of your diaries," I begged. "I want them."

She snorted. "Why would anyone but me want to read those old things?" she asked.

"Because," I told her. "Just because. Please save them for me."

So she did. After Aunt Ruth died, they came to me. I began reading them by starting with the very last one.

Tears came to my eyes at final entry dated May 6, the day she was admitted to a nursing home: "Came to Manor," she wrote, and then her handwriting trailed off on the last word. She died less than a month later.

After that introduction, it took me a few weeks before I could bring myself to look at the rest of the diaries. When I finally sat down to read them, the entries were disappointingly mundane at first glance, mostly emotionless accounts of housework, the weather, the comings and goings of family members, and meetings she attended. Only a few intriguing notations gave a glimpse of her secret soul.

Thursday, April 13, 1933
Cleaned up bedrooms this A.M. Had quite a snowstorm today. Began by raining but everything white tonight except cement. Read the 37th Psalm and such a relief from 3 days of anxiety. Went to prayer meeting and ride afterwards.

From the entries, I traced her life, fascinated by her account of meeting a middle-aged Nazarene preacher, their chaste but clandestine courtship (it wouldn't do to upset the people in the church!), and their eventual marriage when she was in her midforties. Then Aunt Ruth began a life that was more or less devoted to serving others.

When her preacher husband, a World War I veteran suffering from the effects of mustard gas, became frequently ill, she filled in for him as pastor—not in the pulpit but by calling on the sick and elderly, carrying out the day-to-day administration of the church. After he collapsed and died, she immersed herself in the church, playing piano, helping with Bible school, cooking, doing whatever was needed.

Then, sometime in her late eighties, after a career of giving to others, she moved into a high-rise apartment complex for senior citizens. Experimental eye surgery freed her from thick glasses, and she could suddenly see better than she had since she was a girl. No longer hamstrung by her poor eyesight, she could do the fancy crafts and sewing that she so dearly loved to do. It could have been her time to play.

Instead Aunt Ruth chose to become a missionary—of sorts. She collected donated used sheets and towels, cut them up, and stitched them into crib sheets, surgical masks, drapes, hats, and more for a mission hospital in Haiti.

Her legs were starting to betray her now by suddenly letting her down without warning. She could creak around her little apartment, but going out was getting too dangerous. At this point, her entries began to change.

April 4, 1996
Fell in the bathroom. Worked on doctor caps.

And work she did—with a purpose and without financial compensation. Over the next few years, her notations were short, centering around who had come to visit her and how much sewing she had done for the mission. Other entries were concerned with the falls that were becoming more and more frequent, almost as if Satan himself was tripping her up to keep her away from the sewing machine.

She decided she would sew until the sheets quit coming, but for a while there didn't seem to be an end to them. People kept giving her sheets, so Aunt Ruth sewed on. Then in April 1997, just shy of her ninty-fifth birthday, the supply of used sheets suddenly dried up. At this point, she had hand-sewn over 800 separate items for the Haitian mission.

In the year that followed, she sorted out her belongings and began to discard her diaries. It was then that I called her and begged her not to throw them away.

Her possessions had little monetary value; they were mostly old newspaper clippings, tatting thread, books, and assorted family memorabilia. When she died, her total estate was valued at about $1,000. But in addition to the linens, which are still in use to save lives in faraway Haiti, her real fortune is chronicled in her diaries. Like passbook savings accounts, they record the eternal treasures she laid up in heaven by her selfless service to God and others.

Using God's math, the value of a life is not calculated by its duration but by its donation.

Planting for a Bountiful Harvest— Selfless Listening

In his own mad way, Vincent Van Gogh had the right idea—although he demonstrated the concept badly applied when he hacked off his own ear and sent it to a woman he loved—for one of the best gifts you can give another is your ear—though not literally, like poor Vincent!

Listening to another person is not just a lost social grace, but in the cacophony of voices, an attentive ear is sorely needed. If you can stop yourself from touting your own agenda and accomplishments long enough to hear what matters to someone else, you are being truly loving to them.

If you listen with rapt attention to an elderly person tell you the same story you've heard a hundred times before, you are loving him.

If you take time to interpret the lisps of a child, you are loving her.

If you attend to the fears of a friend without discounting their validity, you are loving him.

If you let someone who mourns talk about her loss, you are loving her.

If you respectfully listen to the ideas of a person whom others discount, you are loving him.

If you patiently hear the frustrations of a young person, you are loving her.

In this world where everybody has something to say, few people really listen. Be one of the few who listen, and you will be loving.

A Bitter Harvest— Little Weeds of Selfishness to Beware

Do you. . .

- give money to the Lord to attempt to blackmail Him into blessing you financially?

- mention "prayer requests" as an opportunity to show off how much you know about the lives of others?

- only serve the Lord in high profile positions?

- insist on your own way just to show your family who's boss?

- allow one of Jesus' "little ones" to be hurt in the name of family peace or security?

- look the other way when someone has a need so you won't be inconvenienced?

- welcome a prominent person to your church or social circle while you avoid someone who is not of your economic class?

- hesitate to share the gospel of Jesus Christ because you are afraid your testimony will cost you financially? Or that you will be considered a "religious fanatic"?

- interrupt others to express your own opinion?

- think you're the only one who is right?

- monopolize conversations?

- give the old "silent treatment" to those who have offended you instead of working out your differences?

- point out the faults and failings of others to embarrass them?

- look down on others who are in difficult financial situations, while you never offer to help?

- love selflessly? Unless you do, you do not love at all.

Prayers to the Lord
of the Harvest

Dear Lord,
Help me not to take unfair advantage of others
for personal gain. Help me to understand that if I
give to the poor, You will provide my needs, but if
I hide my eyes from the needy, a curse will be
upon me (Proverbs 28:27). Help me to give
what I have to the poor and lay up my treasures

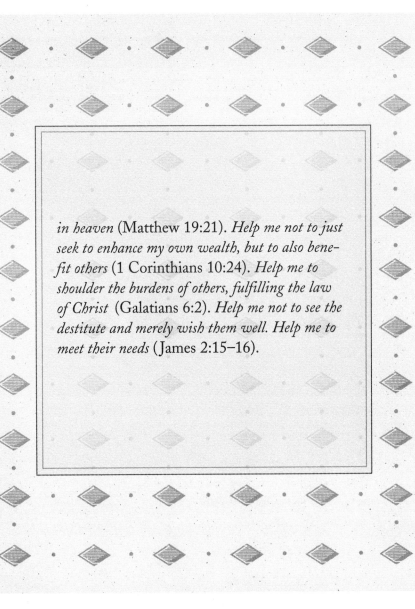

in heaven (Matthew 19:21). *Help me not to just seek to enhance my own wealth, but to also benefit others* (1 Corinthians 10:24). *Help me to shoulder the burdens of others, fulfilling the law of Christ* (Galatians 6:2). *Help me not to see the destitute and merely wish them well. Help me to meet their needs* (James 2:15–16).

Chapter 9

Love Is Not Easily Angered
Planting the Seeds of Patient Love

Love. . .
is not easily angered.

1 CORINTHIANS 13:4–5

Anger is like an onion: It yields layer upon layer of wrath and animosity. What you find at the core is hurt. Courage and tears are needed to peel away the layers, lay bare the secret sorrow, and commit it to God. That is the only way true growth will occur.

Love with Lightning—Out of the Blue

"My parents were like thunder and lightning," said Bert. "Dad yelled around a lot, but it was generally harmless noise. He rarely acted on his anger. Mother, on the other hand, seldom raised her voice. Even when she was angry, she hardly ever yelled. She would patiently correct our indiscretions time and time again. But when she felt she had sufficiently warned us of the consequences of misbehavior, she would discipline us with the swiftness of a lightning bolt out of a clear blue sky. No anger. No yelling. Just pure correction. And we knew she had us dead to rights." He shook his head and grinned. "We tried to never push Mother."

The personality of Bert's mother shaped his impressions of God. "Some people relate God's personality to that of their earthly fathers. Not me. I think God is more like my mother: patient, forgiving, long-suffering—but with a loving lightning bolt ready if I stray too far." He grinned again. "I try to never push God."

Words to Prune By

The man or woman who has a quick temper usually is a person of decisive action. Unfortunately, when anger is in control of the person, it often produces the wrong actions. The person who puts temper under God's control will not only change the world but will conquer it as well.

Cultivating Anger Control

Ask God daily for mastery over anger. Here's a sample prayer:

Dear Father,
Help me to cease from anger
and forsake wrath:
Help me not to agitate myself
in any way to do evil.
Based on PSALM 37:8

Help me to be slow to anger,
for that is better than being mighty.
Help me to rule my spirit,
for that is better than ruling a city.
Based on PROVERBS 16:32

A soft answer turneth away wrath: but grievous words stir up anger.

PROVERBS 15:1

- If you and your loved ones need to be reminded of this verse, consider embroidering or painting it as a wall display for a prominent area in your home.

- Start small. Seek to gain control of your little outbursts of anger. You'll build up "muscles" for controlling the big irritations.

- Before you feel anger rising, pray for empathy, sympathy, and compassion.

He that is slow to wrath is of great understanding.
PROVERBS 14:29

Apologize for out-of-control behavior. It is important that you take responsibility for your behavior and the devastation that it causes.

Love is the grace and power of God working through me in a positive form for the best interest of another person— regardless of his merit. We start to love when we begin to look at our enemy through the eyes of God, for God is love.

CARL V. BINKLEY

"My father-in-law and I were installing storm windows in my house one day," Butch said. "I was a young know-it-all and not very handy with tools, and he was trying to show me what to do. When it came time to put in the second-floor windows, he told me to hang the hammer on my tool belt before I climbed up the ladder with the window.

"I guess I resented being told what to do, so I just tucked it under my arm and up I went. When I went to slide the storm window into place, the hammer slipped from under my arm and conked my father-in-law square on the head. He fell to the ground.

"Needless to say, I scrambled down the ladder and knelt over him. His lips were moving, and when I put my ear to his lips, I could hear him softly counting to ten.

"I'm thankful that both my father-in-law and God are slow to wrath. I'm still a little bit of a know-it-all when it comes to doing things my way instead of God's. Sometimes I think if I could hear the audible voice of God, He'd be saying, 'One. . . two. . .three. . .' "

Love covers. . .a multitude of sins.

1 PETER 4:8 NIV

The person who masters temper is master of everything. And the person who cannot control temper can be controlled by anything.

How to Salvage the Wind-Damaged Fruit of Love

When he was a young pastor at his first charge, Jack had problems with his church organist, Ruth. "She was always late getting to church. In fact, the church board changed the time the service started on Sunday morning to fifteen minutes later, just so Ruth could get there on time. But then she started coming a little later than before!"

Ruth's tardiness irritated Jack. "I was taught in seminary that you start the service on time," he said, "and I believed it was a lie to tell people morning worship was at 9:15 and then start at 9:25. It made the congregation and visitors question the pastor's integrity. I certainly didn't want that, but I couldn't get Ruth to cooperate."

Not only was Ruth always late, but she made a big production out of being late. "She'd come in late, go to the ladies' room, talk to the other latecomers, then run up to the front of the church with her coat still on. Then, in front of the whole congregation, she'd take a little longer to get organized, smiling apologetically the whole time. I thought it was just a power play on her part. She was really getting on my nerves, and I decided something had to be done."

After pondering his alternatives, Jack decided to simply start the service on time. "The next Sunday while Ruth was getting settled, I stood up and said, 'While we're waiting for Ruth, let's stand and sing the first hymn.'

"From the pulpit, I saw Ruth in the back of the church. When she heard the congregation singing without her, her head snapped up and she stared at me with undisguised hurt and rage. Then she grabbed her coat and left. I was without an organist for the rest of the service."

During the next week, the Lord began to work on him about the way he had treated Ruth. "She was wrong—but so was I. I should have followed the scriptural principle of first talking to her about the problem, then if it continued, having some others speak to her, and so on. But I was such a hotshot. I was unloving."

Eventually, God showed Jack what he needed to do: He apologized to Ruth and she forgave him. And she was never late for church again.

When you've hurt someone with your words, apologize—first to God, confessing your lack of love, and then to the person.

*Man will be
controlled by God
or he will be
ruled by tyrants.*

BENJAMIN FRANKLIN

Why do people who give others a "piece of their mind" usually take as much as they give? Because they generally manage to take away their own peace of mind.

You may live with someone who is easily angered. Everyday you may encounter physical, sexual, verbal, emotional, or mental abuse. You understand better than most how the quick-tempered person can leave you feeling lonely and unloved. You know when your abuser lifts his hand or voice to harm you that at that moment, he hates you so much that he would destroy you if he could with a punch or a word.

But there is Someone who loves you, and that person is

Jesus Christ. Ask Him for protection for yourself and others in your household who may also be abused. Ask Him to show you the practical things you need to do to get help. Allow Him to lead you into safety. He does not want you in danger.

Don't be afraid to ask for and accept help. Don't allow the abuse to continue. You are not loving the abuser if you don't make him accept the consequences of his behavior. By refusing to tolerate abuse any longer, you may force your abuser to come to Christ for healing.

Above all, understand that you are loved, regardless of how you feel when the hail of abuse rains down upon your head.

A Prayer to Our Loving Master Gardener

Dear Lord,
protect me from
the killing drought of anger,
both in my life and
in the lives of those around me.

Chapter 10

Love Keeps No Record of Wrongs
Planting the Seeds of Love

Charity. . .

thinketh no evil.

1 Corinthians 13:4–5

Love. . .
keeps no record of wrongs.
1 Corinthians 13:4–5 NIV

"My ability to accept Christ's forgiveness is the direct result of an experience I had on the day I found out I was pregnant," said Amy.

"I was nineteen, unmarried, a sophomore in college, and in denial about all that was wrong with my life. When the doctor told me I was pregnant, I took the car and went to the town where my boyfriend was in college. I told him, and then we called my parents. 'We're coming home,' we told them, 'and we need to talk to you.' "

Her pregnancy did not seem to surprise her parents. Somehow, they had already caught wind of Amy's predicament. "They knew I was pregnant before we got there to tell them, and when we came in, Dad reached out, took my arm, pulled me on his lap, and asked, 'Are you okay?' "

Amy said her father's actions not only surprised her; they touched her to the core of her being. "I expected to be yelled at and told, 'You're a bad girl!' But my dad's love for me wasn't in any way connected to my actions. He just loved me.

"Since then, I've thought a million times of my dad's love — and every time, I can't help but relate it to God's unconditional love. Whenever I blow things in life, my most powerful coping tool is to envision myself crawling up onto my heavenly Father's lap, finding forgiveness, comfort, and acceptance."

If your enemy is hungry,
give him food to eat;
and if he is thirsty,
give him water to drink.

PROVERBS 25:21 NIV

Pruning the Damaged Leaves— Loving the Villains in Your Life

Is there someone who has wronged you? You are in a great position to "love your enemies" and "pray for those who despitefully use you."

How do you pray for them? Because those people have wronged you, you already know some of their worst blemishes—so you can pray for their deliverance from those imperfections.

A prayer if someone has cheated you or lied to you:

Father, help (insert name) to be honest in
Your sight and in the sight of others.

2 CORINTHIANS 7:2

A prayer if someone has been unkind to you:

Father, help (insert name) to be kind to others,
tenderhearted, and forgiving of others, even as
You for Christ's sake have forgiven me.

EPHESIANS 4:32

A prayer if someone has gossiped about you:

Father, give (insert name) the strength of
character to not go up and down as a tale-
bearer among people (Leviticus 19:16), but
develop in (insert name) a faithful spirit.

PROVERBS 11:13

A prayer if someone has humiliated you:

Father, help (insert name) to understand that
You resist the proud but give grace to the
humble. Help (insert name) to be humble in
Your sight so that You may lift up this person.

JAMES 4:6, 10

A prayer if someone hates you:

> Father, let all bitterness and wrath, and anger,
> and clamor, and evil speaking be put away
> from (insert name).   EPHESIANS 4:31

A prayer if someone has been unfaithful to you:

> Create in (insert name) a clean heart, O God;
> and renew a right spirit in (insert name).
>
>   PSALM 51:11

Enjoying the Fruit of Forgiveness

All of us want forgiveness—but some of us have trouble forgiving. However, God's Word is clear: Unless we freely forgive, we won't be forgiven. But if we can bring ourselves to bless our enemies, God will reward us. That is the fruit forgiveness yields.

Blessed are the merciful: for they shall obtain mercy.

MATTHEW 5:7

A Fragile Fruit—Forgiving Forever

"When I opened the December telephone bill and it read $1,500 plus, I couldn't believe my eyes!" said Karen. "Although I use the phone a lot with my business, I try to keep the bills up-to-date. This was ridiculous!"

Karen needed to do only a small amount of detective work to discover a list of overseas phone calls made from her number to all sorts of places: Haiti, Guyana, and African countries Karen had never heard of.

"I pulled out the previous month's bill and there were a bunch on there, too. I'd just paid the amount and not looked too closely, but some of these calls cost $50 a minute!"

As Karen and her husband questioned everyone in the house, suspicion fell heavily on their fourteen-year-old son. He had been in trouble quite a lot lately—and he finally admitted that he was responsible for the calls.

He had seen an infomercial about pills that were reputed to "melt off fat and build muscle." When he called the toll-free number on the screen, an automated answering service had offered him a number of other options, some of which were adult entertainment lines. The recording told him to press star and a digit; in his excitement, he missed the information that he would pay overseas rates. Before he knew it, he had racked up a huge bill, all without talking to anyone but automated answering services.

Said Karen: "My husband downloaded a lot of information off the Internet that was helpful, but I still spent hours on the telephone talking to a host of long-distance companies, some of which were cooperative and some of which were not. Our son didn't realize it, but this was twice the amount we were planning to spend on Christmas presents for the entire family! Now, I wasn't even sure we could purchase gifts."

Karen had to fight the tide of resentment that was rising within her.

"He was very sorry about it. And while he knew he shouldn't have been on the phone with adult sex lines, I knew it was partially an accident that he was tempted to get on them in the first place. But I still wanted to wring his neck! I wanted to keep reminding him of his offenses, because it was taking several days of my time and a lot of money to clear them up."

Karen got $1,260 hacked off her bill—but she still had to pray about her attitude. "I wanted our son to never forget what he did—but I also wanted him to learn about God's forgiveness through our forgiveness. Then God showed me what to do. I wrote 'forgiven' on the bills, tied them with a big bow, and put them in his Christmas stocking.

"We had a smaller-than-normal Christmas, but I think our fourteen-year-old truly understood grace for the first time," said Karen.

Impaled on Your Own Thorns—
When You Are the Villain

When you look back on your life and see that you have been your own worst enemy, you may say you've accepted God's forgiveness—but have you forgiven yourself?

Tracey bitterly hated someone and she could not forgive her. That person was herself. "I hated myself because of some things I did in high school and just after I graduated. I got pregnant several times by different guys and I had a series of abortions.

"At first, the abortions didn't bother me. I thought, 'If the government says abortion is legal, then it can't be morally wrong.' I knew having sex with a bunch of different guys was wrong even though it was legal, but I didn't transfer that same logic to the abortions. You see, I had to work real hard to justify them to myself."

The fifth abortion she had made her come face-to-face with the reality of what she had done. "I went down to one of those women's clinics for this last abortion. They did it and I thought it was all over with. But then I noticed that the symptoms of pregnancy weren't going away. *I can't be pregnant,* I thought; *I had an abortion.*

"It turned out that it wasn't a complete abortion. I was still pregnant, and by now I was about five months along."

Tracey went back to the clinic. They showed her the paper she had signed absolving them of any responsibility, and then they set up an appointment for her at another clinic to finish the abortion. "It was really weird and creepy," Tracey remembered. "The doctor let me into the clinic after hours and it was just him and me. He didn't use any anesthetic and it was extremely painful and bloody.

"When he was done and was checking to see if he'd got it all, I first started hearing the voice. It was a child's voice asking, 'Why did you kill me? Why did you hate me? I would have loved you.'"

Although Tracey could get rid of the unwanted baby, she couldn't get rid of the questioning voice during the day or at night. "I couldn't sleep, because I'd dream about a baby asking me, 'Why did you kill me? Why did you hate me?' I'd start to run and the baby would float behind me asking, 'Why did you kill me? Why did you hate me?' I would run all night in my sleep, but I couldn't get away from it."

Oftentimes during the day she would also hear that small, questioning voice. Then the voice was joined by a chorus of tiny questioning voices that she recognized as the other babies she had aborted. Tracey began to consider suicide.

"Night after night, I was chased through my nightmares by these little babies and their voices. The counselor called it 'post-abortion trauma,' and said I would need extensive psychiatric treatment. I wasn't a Christian then, but I knew what I really needed was God's forgiveness and the forgiveness of my aborted children. I didn't think God could possibly forgive me, though."

A work friend who had been witnessing to Tracey told her the stories of David's guilt in Uriah's murder, how Moses had murdered an Egyptian, and that the apostle Paul, formerly Saul, had been responsible for the deaths of many Christians in the early church. "She told me that if God could forgive them, He could forgive me. I prayed the sinner's prayer with her. I've never had such a release in my spirit!" said Tracey.

Her friend's pastor held a memorial service for Tracey's lost babies. At the service, Tracey read a letter to them, apologizing for taking their lives. She promised to see them in heaven.

"Mother's Day and the anniversaries of the abortions are still painful. Forgiving myself is so hard. Sometimes, when I start to feel condemned for what I did, I tell myself, 'No! God's forgiven me! He promised to forgive and forget my sins! If God can do that, then I will do the same.'"

The "Golden Rule" instructs us to be kind to others as well as ourselves. If God wants us to forgive others, that means He wants us to forgive ourselves too.

The second greatest commandment not only requires that we love our neighbor, but also that we love ourselves (Mark 12:31).

Entangling Vines

One day as I put away groceries, I observed my cat Emily playing in one of the discarded plastic bags. She was having a great time pouncing around looking for the elusive rustling sounds. Amused with her antics, I threw a couple of cat treats in the bag to make it even more interesting for both her and me.

She eventually exhausted herself and sat in the bag peering at me through the handle loop. I smiled at her I'm-pretending-to-be-a-lion-in-a-cave look. Then, for no discernable reason, she suddenly made a lunge through the bag opening and caught her head in the loop. As she ran through the house, the bag filled up with air and "chased" her. She panicked and raced madly about while I tried vainly to catch her. She had done something to cause this plastic apparition to haunt her, and now she didn't know how to get away from it.

However, if she had the opportunity to play with a bag again she would take it in a heartbeat! (Okay, she is not smart, just cute and cuddly!)

Like a cat caught in a bag handle, you can't easily get away from yourself or your actions. Who and what you are will pursue you twenty-four hours a day. Your past will hound you, haunt you, and hamper you—unless you let God release you from it.

Sowing Seeds of Love and Forgiveness— for Ourselves

"I hate myself!"

Oftentimes when a child does something wrong and they are reaping the consequences, they will make that statement. As a parent, the words cause great pain, because you have made that child. When they say they hate themselves, they are saying they hate you.

As an individual made by God, when we say we hate ourselves, we're saying we hate Him.

You should love yourself when you have done wrong, just as you should love others when they fail—because somewhere in all of us is the image of God. That is the part you should love.

Once you learn that God loves you and forgives every sin, you can begin to love and accept yourself. If God forgives you, you have no right to hold a grudge against yourself.

Chapter 11

Love Does Not Delight in Evil
Planting the Seeds of a Love-Filled Life

Love does not delight in evil.

1 CORINTHIANS 13:6 NIV

One of the queer characteristics of human nature is that we often would rather hear of someone's misfortune than his or her successes.

Help from the
Master Gardener
A Prayer

Dear Lord,
Thank You that Your love keeps no record of all
my wrongs. Help me to walk out in the freedom
of Your love, forgiving myself. And may I as
freely forgive those around me. Let me never hold
a grudge, but fill me full of committed, uncondi-
tional love.

Love Blooms in Winter's Chill
The Valentine Secret

As I was planning a Valentine's party for the senior citizens' group at church, I asked some of the married couples to bring wedding photos. I made the photos into slides to become a guessing game: Who Is This Handsome Couple?

I was curious to see the wedding pictures of one couple in particular—Bob and Helen. I wanted to see what they looked like when they were happy with each other—for they certainly weren't anymore.

Bob and Helen's marriage was more a study in gritty endurance than a picture of romance. They had known each other all their lives; they had even attended the same one-room school. But before they were a couple, Bob had been their friend Alma's beau.

The change occurred one fateful summer long ago when Alma went to visit relatives and asked her best friend Helen to "take care" of Bob while she was gone. When she returned, Bob and Helen broke the news: They were in love. They were going to be married. They were sorry.

And they were sorry for sixty years, for their marriage was miserable. Sometime, while tending his farm or looking at Helen across the breakfast table, Bob realized that he still loved Alma. He never said it, but Helen knew it.

Not that they didn't try to be happy. During a short season

of détente, they produced a family. Then the war commenced in earnest.

While they fought on, Alma never forgot Bob. How could she? She taught his children both in Sunday school and public school. She sat alone behind Bob and Helen in church. She worked on countless committees with Helen, served potluck dinners with her, sang in the choir with both of them, and never said a word to anyone about her broken heart. She quietly, gracefully, grew older, then grayer, and finally retired, still alone.

Over the years, Helen and Bob's marriage grew increasingly acrimonious. Sometime after their children left the nest, they quit speaking to one another altogether. Bob worked the farm; Helen cleaned the house and fixed his meals, but because they couldn't be civil to one another, a word didn't pass between them.

Friends had long ago forgotten that Alma and Bob were ever an item, but the fact that Bob and Helen didn't speak was an interesting open secret. Everyone knew. Including Alma.

So when the slide of Helen and Bob's 1928 wedding flashed up on the screen, Alma caught her breath, creaked to her feet, and shuffled off to the ladies' rest room, sobbing with ancient heartbreak. I found her there and heard the story.

Eyes streaming, she said, "It hurt to lose Bob. But the thing that has hurt me far more has been knowing that my two dearest friends were so unhappy."

She had truly loved.

Godly love does not take entertainment
in the misfortunes of others.
It mourns with those who mourn
and rejoices with those who rejoice.
Love is not merely a euphoric emotion,
for our emotions fade, change, or fail.
God's love never fades or fails.
Love is the supernatural grace
of God flowing through me—
sometimes with my joyful consent,
sometimes with a disciplined,
committed act of my will—
to promote the best interests
of all I encounter,
be they friends or foes—
often without an appreciative response.

CARL V. BINKLEY

A HARVEST OF LOVE

"I have a prayer request," she said, then proceeded to give a salacious account about two people, resplendent with the details of their moral lapse. Was her Christian love only feigned? While she didn't want to be an out-and-out gossip, was the story just too good to keep to herself?

"She asked me to keep this confidential," he said, "but I knew you would be concerned and maybe you could offer help." Was this breach of confidence justified?

"So how are you bearing up since your problems?" he asked. Was he really interested? Or did he just want to know the gruesome details so he could pass them on?

"How are you really, dear?" she asked. Did she care? Or was she just looking for a "scoop"?

Love is careful with the details of other people's lives.

Love does not betray secrets.

When asked to pray for someone, love promises and then prays.

Love does not ask out of curiosity but out of concern.

A Prayer for
a Heart of Love

Lord,
Keep my heart from delighting in gossip and my
tongue from spreading it.

When I know that my brother or sister is
overtaken in sin, remind me to pray rather than
talk about the problem, knowing that You will
cut off those who secretly slander their neighbors

(Psalm 101:5). *Let me lay aside all malicious talk and all duplicity and hypocrisies and enviousness and all evil speech* (1 Peter 2:1).

I know that out of the abundance of my heart, my mouth speaks, so I ask that You cleanse my heart of hatred and evil. I want to bring forth a treasure of love rather than an overflow of evil.

Chapter 12

Love Rejoices with the Truth
Planting Seeds of Truthful Love

Love. . .

rejoices with the truth.

1 Corinthians 13:4, 6 NIV

An honest answer is like a kiss on the lips.

Proverbs 24:26 NIV

Do You Love Enough?

Would you be angry with me if I told you that you have bad breath in the morning? Or would you say, "Thanks!" and go brush your teeth?

Would you be angry with me if I told you that you have a nervous habit that drives people up the wall? Or would you say, "Stop me the next time you see me do that"—and not snap at me when I do?

Would you be angry with me if I corrected your grammar in private? Or would you say, "I appreciate that you don't want me to look like a fool"?

Would you be angry with me if you discovered my faults? Or would you say, "Let me pray with you" and love me anyway?

Frost Makes the Love Grow
Tough Love

Angie was uncertain how to answer her friend Steve's persistent question.

"He was always asking me, 'Why don't women like me?' Then he would go through this long list of all of his lady-killer qualifications: 'I'm not bad-looking.' 'I have a good income.'

'I'm polite.' 'I have a good sense of humor.' 'I'm intelligent.' After a while, I wanted to scream!

"I knew why women didn't like Steve. The reason was simple: He was totally self-centered! He never talked about anybody but himself. I could spend a whole day with him and he'd never ask me anything about myself."

Angie prayed about how to answer Steve's question.

"He was so lonely and I knew I and a few of the people in the church singles' group were about his only friends—and he got on *our* nerves! I felt sorry for him. He was already hurting and I didn't want to cause him any more pain, but I didn't feel like it was right to let him go on like he was. I kept praying that God would help him to be less self-centered so I wouldn't have to say anything."

But Angie felt God urging her to speak.

"After I prayed about it, one day the Holy Spirit put His elbow in my ribs, gave me a good nudge, and said, 'Tell him!' So I did."

She tried to be gentle, but Steve was angry with her. "God maybe could have used somebody with more tact than me, but He must have wanted a direct approach. Steve didn't speak to me for a couple of weeks, but then out of the blue he called, apologized, and thanked me. He said that he had started listening to himself talk, and he'd realized what a huge bore he must have been to other people.

"Even if he hadn't apologized, though, telling him was still the right thing to do. I wouldn't have been acting in love if I'd let him go through life wondering why people weren't responding to him."

Better is an open rebuke
than hidden love.
Wounds from a friend
can be trusted,
but an enemy
multiplies kisses.

PROVERBS 27:5–6 NIV

Mark and Martha were undecided whether or not to leave their sixteen-year-old daughter Jessica alone while they went away overnight.

"Of our two children, Jessica was usually the responsible one, and she knew our ground rules," said Martha.

Leaving her with a list of chores, Mark and Martha waved good-bye to Jessica but not without some trepidation.

"I was nervous," said Martha, "but she assured us that she would be fine."

Jessica's main chore would be to mow the yard, a task she could complete in less than a half hour. But when Mark and Martha pulled back in their driveway, Jessica had obviously not even begun the job. Inside their home, Jessica was in bed, sleeping soundly, looking exhausted.

Said Martha: "My first thought was that she was sick, so we tiptoed out and let her sleep."

But then Martha accidentally stumbled across a beer can under the bathroom sink. "Right away, I guessed what had happened. I wanted to go into Jessica's bedroom and shake her until her teeth rattled!"

Instead, she walked next door and asked her neighbor if anything had happened while they were gone. The story the neighbor told did not make Martha happy. Jessica had indeed hosted a large party at Mark and Martha's house. The neighbor said the police had been called to the premises. After Martha called the police to verify their visit, she was ready to confront Jessica.

"I was so angry, but the Lord kept saying to me, 'Love her as I have loved you in your rebellion.' So I waited until she got up, and then I calmly asked her how she got along while we were gone."

At first, Jessica was evasive and dishonest, but when Martha handed her the beer can, Jessica confessed the whole story. "I was so glad that she came out with the truth. I put my arms around her and told her, 'No matter what you've done, you can always tell me. It doesn't mean I won't punish you, but it means I'll always forgive you.'

"She told her dad when he came in—and then we had such a precious time together. She was grounded for a month, but because she knew we loved her enough to accept her—disobedience and all—the incident paved the way for a better relationship."

Words that nourish the soul are carefully seasoned with both love and honesty.

Growing Honest Love

When Barbara heard that her young cousin Pam was planning a hasty marriage with Ed, a man she had only known for a few weeks, Barbara felt she needed to speak up although she hated to interfere. "I knew for some reason Ed must be pressuring her into making such a quick decision," said Barbara, "but she barely knew him. They had met on the Internet, and they hadn't even been out on a date! I didn't feel that I could just let her walk into this without saying something."

Barbara waited for an opportunity to talk to Pam alone, but she knew she'd have to do it quickly since the wedding was fast approaching. Her only opportunity came after a Sunday dinner when Barbara, Pam, and two of their aunts were alone in the kitchen clearing up the dishes.

"I tried to tell her that she didn't have to rush into this marriage with Ed," said Barbara, "but oddly enough, although my aunts had agreed with me in private, now they tried to shut me up. One of them said, 'If we don't just accept what she wants to do, she won't tell us anything.'

"I just didn't agree. I thought speaking up and encouraging her to wait was the right thing to do, so I did it."

Despite Barbara's objections, Pam went ahead with the marriage. Not surprisingly, the marriage had problems almost from the start. Embarrassed by her actions and in trouble, Pam didn't know where to turn for comfort or help. When she explained her situation to a friend, the friend advised, "Talk to your cousin. You may not have liked it when she tried to stop you from getting married, but you know that she loved you because she told you the truth!"

Today, Pam's situation is not good and a divorce seems inevitable, but Barbara has never said "I told you so" to Pam. "I've certainly made mistakes in my life, too, but I told her the truth in love because I wanted to help her, not just be the cousin who knows it all," said Barbara. "And now I plan to keep right on doing all I can to show her I love her, no matter what decision she makes from here."

Love Rooted in Truth
Repairing the Damage of Unfaithfulness

Laura did not know how to tell Rich she had been unfaithful to him, so she decided not to bring it up. But she also decided if he ever asked her, she'd tell him the truth—something she had never done before.

"God had been working in my life and I knew what I had done was wrong. I knew it at the time. We married very young and Rich was very irresponsible in those days, but that does not excuse my behavior. I was irresponsible, too. Rich suspected that I'd had love affairs, but whenever he asked, I always told him 'no' because I didn't think he'd love me if I told him the truth," said Laura.

"One day we were having an argument. Rich just flat out asked me. So I told him."

The fallout from her answer surprised both Laura and Rich. It opened the door for the first honest discussion they had had for many years.

"I had withheld all kinds of information from Rich—about finances, emotions, you name it—because in the past he really flipped out when there were any problems," said Laura. "He'd ask me, 'What's wrong?' and I'd say, 'Nothing'—when the truth was that we were in terrible financial shape or I was worried about something else. My lack of honesty slowly closed the door on intimacy. I didn't think he could handle the truth. I resented having to protect him from life, but what I was really doing was keeping him a child."

This couple reaped a whole load of trouble because of Laura's lack of honesty with Rich.

"I didn't trust his love for me. I thought he'd leave me if he knew how bad the situation was. Maybe he would have," admitted Laura, "but God showed me I was responsible for my actions, not Rich's reactions.

"If I loved Rich, I had to be honest with him. I don't mean bludgeon Rich with the truth, but I had to speak the truth in love."

You may not need to confess "big sins" to your loved ones, and you may not need to confront them on anything major. But we all have areas in our lives where we are less than honest. Even the smallest evasion of the truth erects a wall between people.

The love of Christ wants to tear down walls. Only then can we all be one in His Spirit.

Help from the
Master Gardener
A Prayer

Lord,
help me to always speak
the truth in love.
Create in me
a spirit of loving honesty.

Chapter 13

Love Protects
Seeds of Love's Protection

Love. . .

always protects.

1 CORINTHIANS 13:6–7 NIV

Love does not drag flaws and faults into the light of day to ridicule them, but quietly and privately seeks to mend them.

"I was always glad that the people on my father's side of the family lived to be very old—until Dad's mind started to slip," said Margaret. "He and I had always been close, and I thought I knew Dad. I never dreamed that he would get like he did in his old age!"

Her father had once been a dapper older gentleman, financially well off after retiring from management of his own company. "After Mom died," said Margaret, "oh, several years later, Dad started pursuing women. At first, I thought he was just lonely and looking for companionship or a new wife, but it became obvious that he wasn't simply seeking companionship. He was saying and doing things that were just plain obscene!"

Margaret spoke to her father several times about his strange, new proclivities. She asked him to behave himself, but he was unrepentant.

"I wasn't sure what to do with him. That was taken out of my hands when the police called one evening. They had arrested Dad on an indecent exposure charge! My eighty-seven-year-old father was a proverbial dirty old man!"

Police told Margaret they had received a number of complaints about her father's inappropriate behavior, but since he was well-known and respected in the community, they had looked the other way—until now. Clearly Margaret would have to act.

"It was so painful to have my father declared incompetent. He didn't understand it either. He was mad at me! But he had nearly emptied all of his bank accounts sending gifts to women he didn't know!"

Confined to a nursing home, Margaret's dad still was obsessed with sex, but he became angry and mean also. "In those days, they called it 'hardening of the arteries,' but it was probably a form of Alzheimer's disease. Physically, he was just fine; mentally, he was a mess. When he recognized me, he was mad at me because I'd put him there. When he didn't know me, he made sexual overtures toward me. It was awful to see how this wonderful, intelligent man had changed!

"I tried to remember Dad as he was before. I made decisions based on my love for that person instead of my feelings for this strange little man who tried to pinch the nurses' aids. Today I tell my children about the man he used to be rather than the one he became. The Bible teaches that we should respect our parents—and the best way I could do that was to protect Dad from himself."

Margaret's love was strong enough to cover even her father's ugly change in personality. Is your love for others as strong? Or is it dependent on them making you feel good?

When you see someone's private flaws, the law of love asks that you still respect that person. After all, isn't that what you'd like someone to do who saw your faults?

The Protective Language of Love

- ◆ Love unobtrusively says, "Your pants are unzipped."
- ◆ Love quietly whispers, "You need a breath mint."
- ◆ Love gently suggests, "Let's go on a diet and do some exercises together."
- ◆ Love diplomatically says, "No, I don't think that outfit flatters your figure."
- ◆ Love privately mentions, "You have lipstick on your teeth and mascara smeared under your eyes."
- ◆ Love acknowledges, "Yes, I've heard you give better speeches."
- ◆ Love says, "Let me help you with your addiction."
- ◆ Love confidentially discloses, "I saw your under-age child hanging out with bad company. May I pray with you for your child?"
- ◆ Love tells an older parent, "Your driving is

endangering someone I love—you. It's time to hang up the keys."

- Love tells a child, "No," even when "All the kids are going!"
- Love asks, "How's your walk with the Lord?"

True Love, Real Protection

Jack was delighted with the birth of his son. He looked forward to teaching the little boy all kinds of things. But first he discovered he had to teach him what "no" meant.

Jack recalled: "He was just starting to walk and he wanted to pull himself up by the drapes. If he had, he might have yanked them down on his head."

Jack got down on the floor with his small son, and each time the child reached for the drape, he firmly told the child "No" and removed his pudgy hand from the curtain. "It took the better part of a half hour, but he learned that when I said 'no' I meant it. It was time well spent that kept him from getting hurt."

Love is a positive action.
Love is to see
another person's problem—
and if it is within your power—
to do what you can to alleviate it.

CARL V. BINKLEY

Strong Love

"But all the kids watch that program," Danny protested to his mother.

Said Susan: "I knew that was mostly true. I knew that the TV show was very popular—but I also knew that it had lots of scary, satanic images in it and that Danny is very impressionable. Some kids can sort reality from fantasy at an early age; most can't and Danny can't. However, I hated to keep Danny from watching it when all of his friends would be. Against my better judgment, I let him watch the program."

Later that night as Susan slept, Danny slipped into bed next to her.

"What's wrong?" she asked.

"I'm scared," he told her.

Susan's husband needed his sleep, so she took Danny into his own bed and lay down there with him. Susan said her hair was hanging off of the bed, but Danny reached over and pulled it up on the mattress.

"Don't let your hair hang down there," he told her. "They might reach up and pull you under!"

"Who?" Susan asked.

"The monsters under the bed," Danny told her.

At that moment, Susan knew her stand against scary programs was right—no matter how much Danny protested. "I held him and apologized for letting him watch that program. I told him, 'I should have better protected your mind.' He forgave me and agreed he shouldn't have watched it.

"Of course the next afternoon when that program came on, he wanted to watch it again. He threw a big fit because I wouldn't let him! But I told him, 'I love you too much to let your mind be messed up.'

"Now that he's older, we're still battling over these issues, but his heart and mind are too important to surrender to the devil's messages. Danny can be angry at me all he wants. He can throw all the fits he wants. I'll still protect him as long as I can."

The Loving Fruit of Protection

It is a hard for a little girl to realize that her father does not love her. Georgia was about four when she came to that realization.

An alcoholic, Georgia's dad was terrifyingly cruel. Abusive when drunk and neglectful when sober, he took a sadistic pleasure out of forcing Georgia to do things he knew she feared.

"He knew I was afraid of chickens, so he would make me carry them into the chicken coop by their feet. I would get flapped and pecked and he would laugh. I was only about four years old at the time.

"I wanted a father like I saw other girls have, one that would protect me and buy me little gifts. Most of all, I wanted a father who would keep his hands to himself."

One day, Georgia told her mother what her father was doing to her. Although she had five children, she took them and left to protect Georgia.

"After that, my aunts came to our house to take us kids to church," Georgia remembers. "It was there I learned about my Father in heaven. I realized that God was the Father that I'd never have on earth. Even though my earthly father never took care of me, my heavenly Father would."

Our heavenly Father's love never fails us. Like all children, sometimes we may wish He'd give us our own way. But His love is great enough to protect us from the dangers we see as well as the hazards we are too blind to even glimpse.

◈

Only Eternity Will Tell the Rest of the Story

Do you remember that job you desperately wanted but didn't get?

Do you remember that car that pulled out in front of you and drove slowly for miles and miles in a location where you couldn't pass?

Do you remember the appointment you were late for because of a last-minute phone call?

Do you remember that person you really wanted to date but never did?

Do you remember when you were unexpectedly fired from a job?

Do you remember the highway exit ramp you looked for and somehow drove right past?

Do you remember the airline flight you couldn't get?

Do you remember the traffic jam that took so long to clear it threw your whole day off schedule?

You may never know until eternity how God lovingly protected you.

Sometimes what looks like punishment to us is really protection.

My son, do not make light of the
Lord's discipline,
and do not lose heart when
he rebukes you,
because the Lord disciplines
those he loves,
and he punishes everyone
he accepts as a son.

<small>HEBREWS 12:5–6 NIV</small>

A HARVEST OF LOVE

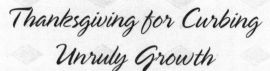

Thanksgiving for Curbing Unruly Growth
A Prayer

Dear Lord,

I confess I don't like it much when You prune my branches or block what looks like the best way for me to grow. But I know in eternity I will see the ways Your love protected me, even when I was too blind to see the danger. Help me never to forget that true love protects.

Chapter 14

Love Always Trusts
Planting the Seeds of Loving Trust

Charity. . .

believeth all things.

1 CORINTHIANS 13:4, 7

Love. . .always trusts.
1 CORINTHIANS 13:6–7 NIV

Planting Trust in God
To Know God Is to Trust Him

It is better to
trust in the LORD
than to put confidence in man.
It is better to
trust in the LORD
than to put confidence in princes.

PSALM 118:8–9

Love trusts that whatever pain God allows you to experience is necessary.

> *Trust in the LORD with all thine heart; and lean not unto thine own understanding. In all thy ways acknowledge him, and he shall direct thy paths.* PROVERBS 3:5–6

Love trusts that God will vigorously defend His people.
*Let all those that put their trust in thee rejoice: let them
ever shout for joy, because thou defendest them.*

PSALM 5:11

Love trusts that God will protect His people.
Whoso putteth his trust in the LORD shall be safe.

PROVERBS 28:25

He is a shield unto them that put their trust in him.

PROVERBS 30:5

Love trusts that God will move mountains for them.
*"I say unto you, That whosoever shall say unto this
mountain, Be thou removed, and be thou cast into the sea;
and shall not doubt in his heart, but shall believe that
those things which he saith shall come to pass; he shall
have whatsoever he saith."* MARK 11:23–24

Love trusts that God will give eternal life.
*"I am the resurrection, and the life: he that believeth in me,
though he were dead, yet shall he live: And whosoever
liveth and believeth in me shall never die."* JOHN 11:25

A HARVEST OF LOVE

Trusting Through the Winter— God's Loving Provision

Nineteen eighty was a very difficult year for my family. I felt like Job. Our children were very young, and although their day-to-day financial needs were small, our expenses that year were staggering because each of us had been hospitalized for unrelated illnesses. Even with insurance, we'd chalked up some hefty medical bills. On top of that, we had had a fire with damage. And the biggest financial load, the heaviest emotional burden of all: We had paid for the funeral of one of our children.

With all this strain, I had lost my health. The doctor told me if I didn't quit my part-time job, my life was at risk. And my husband was unemployed.

I couldn't bring myself to let anyone know how difficult our condition was. Food wasn't a big problem, because earlier that year I had canned our own homegrown chickens, fruit, and vegetables, and we could rely on those. To bridge the gaps, I sold some of our furniture and the best of my doll collection. But as the tight times continued, I was running out of resources and saleable items.

Then the month of December came, and with it, Christmas catalogs and flyers. My heart heavy, I watched the children pore over them with excited anticipation. "Mama!" they would shout, "look at this!" Then they would proceed to show me something wonderful, something we couldn't afford because we couldn't afford anything. As Christmas grew closer, their tastes became more discriminating; they settled down to one "gotta have" item each.

At that point, I really didn't care if they wanted one item or a thousand: There just wasn't any extra money.

When I was putting my husband through college, I'd had some practice with squeezing a penny until Lincoln screamed. But now our financial situation was even tighter than it had been then. I began the practice of spreading our bills out before the Lord, getting on my knees, and not getting up until I had God's assurance that our needs would be met.

God had always come through for us, so I not only had practice at budgeting, but I also had practice trusting Him. In the past, He had blessed us so much that when my husband finished college, we didn't owe a dime. We even had enough to put half down on a house trailer.

So now I just kept praying. And trusting.

One day as Christmas neared, I pushed a cart through the aisles of the large discount grocery/department store where I did my shopping. My eye fell on an entry box for a $25 gift certificate drawing. The box was fairly large and stuffed full of slips signed with people's names. The chances of me winning were very slim, but $25 seemed like a princely amount at that moment, so I signed my name to a form. As I held the entry form in my hand, I prayed, "Lord, I'm not asking to win; I'm just asking You to provide." I wedged the paper into the slot.

As I turned to walk away, it was as if the Spirit of God said to me, "Trust Me. I love you. I'm going to provide for you and your children. I gave the best Gift at the first Christmas; I can certainly take care of gifts for this one. Let Me provide that—and anything else you might need."

I never gave the drawing another thought, but I never doubted God would provide.

I went home and made a modest Christmas list. In addition to socks and underwear for the kids, it included one toy each. I estimated the total cost to be about $40. "Here, Lord," I prayed; "please provide these things."

About a week before Christmas, I got a call from the department store. I had indeed won the $25 gift certificate!

I drove over to the store, list in hand, claimed the certificate, and traveled through the store to pick up as many things on my list as the money would cover. To my amazement, every item on the list was on sale! I kept a running tally of the costs for each item, and when I had selected everything, I still had a little money left. When I figured the remainder, I could buy a string of Christmas lights—and still put $2.50 in the offering plate.

Trusting in God's love is hard when your circumstances seem overwhelming. You may wonder if God cares, but He does. He truly does!

Tilling the Soil
Remembering the Love of God

- The love of God prompted Him to give Adam a woman who was his soul mate. You can trust God to lovingly provide a mate for you.

- The love of God spared Noah and his family in the flood. You can trust God to lovingly care for you in the midst of disaster.

- The love of God gave a promised son to Abraham and Sarah, even though they were very old. You can trust God to lovingly keep His promises.

- The love of God delivered Joseph from prison so he could save the lives of his family. You can trust God to lovingly restore your family circle, too.

- The love of God brought the Israelites out of slavery. You can trust God to lovingly deliver you from the bondage of your sins and past.

- The love of God made a path of dry land through the Red Sea so that the Israelites could escape the

A HARVEST OF LOVE

Egyptian army. You can trust God to lovingly make a plain way for you in times of trouble.

- The love of God brought the Israelites through the wilderness into the Promised Land. You can trust God to lovingly take you through this life to a home in heaven.

- The love of God sent His only begotten Son to earth to die for our sins. You can trust His love.

A Prayer to the Lord of the Harvest

Dear Jesus,
I know that all things are possible to those who believe in You. So like the father who brought his ailing son to You, I ask you to help my unbelief (Mark 9:23–24).

Help me to remember that You are good, a stronghold in the day of trouble (NAHUM 1:7).

Trusting Other People—
A Difficult Plant to Grow

There are two schools of thought on trusting other people.

The first believes you should be skeptical of everyone until they earn your trust. Be wary of these people. Because they are often untrustworthy, they assume others will be, too.

The second believes you should give everyone the benefit of the doubt. That doesn't mean you should hand people your wallet and tell them to help themselves, but it does mean you can assume they mean well. You are a person of goodwill yourself, and you count on God to be your Defender.

The Thorn That Chokes Trust
Hoeing Out the Thorns

I've been hurt. How do I trust again?

Many victims are totally self-absorbed with their pain. If that is you, understand that you aren't the first or the only person to have been betrayed by someone you trusted. Until you come to the point where you can see that your experience is common to all humanity, you'll endlessly whine and lick your wounds while praying for revenge. Other people have been hurt, too, and went on to love again. You can also.

You also have to realize you are not responsible for your victimization.

Jesus, fully God and the perfect Man, had His trust violated. At one point, His family thought He was insane. Later, Judas betrayed Him to His enemies, all of His disciples ran and hid when He was arrested, and Peter denied Him. The same crowds who shouted "Hosanna!" were the crowds who shouted "Crucify Him!" a scant week later. Did He bring this upon Himself? No! The sooner you stop blaming yourself, the sooner you'll heal.

What makes you think you have to trust again? Are you sure God wants you to place your trust in a particular person?

If you know that your husband is a philanderer, that your child can't be trusted with scissors, or that your wife plus a credit card equals financial disaster, don't put him or her into positions that compromise their ability to resist temptation. Don't pretend the weaknesses don't exist. Love them in spite of their flaws. Pray and work toward their recovery. Jesus told us to be as harmless as doves—but He also said we should be as wily as serpents. He expects us to use our common sense—and He doesn't expect us to be doormats laid out for the misuse of others.

Ask God to bring something good out of the pain of the betrayal. God, the Great Salvager, is very good at this. Look at what He did with the crucifixion of Jesus. He used it to reconcile the world to Himself.

How do you trust someone again who has hurt you?
Not easily! The only way is to allow God to love the person through you, relying upon Him to care for your best interests. In other words: Revenge is out! Blessing is in!

Jesus said, "Ye have heard that it hath been said, Thou shalt love thy neighbour, and hate thine enemy. But I say unto you, Love your enemies, bless them that curse you, do good to them that hate you, and pray for them which despitefully use you, and persecute you (Matthew 5:43–44)."

You know and understand the world's ethics: Love your friends; hate your enemies. However, if you plan to be unconditionally true to Christ, you will not look at the present reward of getting your pound of flesh but at eternal joy of seeing your enemies in heaven. Will you clutch at enjoyment and personal benefit here? Or will you relinquish your "rights" to follow Jesus?

If you take the world's way, you must forsake Jesus. If you take Christ's way, you must forsake the world.

But again, that doesn't mean you must be stupid. If you know someone has a weakness, don't tempt them to fall. Avoid enabling them by facilitating temptation. You may not realistically be able to ever trust them again in certain areas—but you *can* love and trust them in their areas of strength. Just don't judge their worth by their areas of **weakness.**

Loving trust does not mean that you are a pushover. It doesn't mean that you are a fool or that you should allow yourself to be exploited. It does mean that you are patient with the flaws of others and that you love them in spite of their flaws. It means you actively seek to help others overcome those flaws, because with your God-given eyes of love, you can see what they can become—once they fill up the sinkholes in their lives!

A Prayer to the Master Gardener

Dear Lord,

Give me the courage to trust others, even though I have been hurt in the past. Help me to rely on Your loving protection when I am vulnerable; remind me that no one can truly harm me if I am Yours. Give me wisdom with those around me, so that I do not place my trust foolishly. May I never put my trust in anyone more than I do in You.

Chapter 15

Love Never Fails
Planting Seeds of Persistent Love

Love. . .

always perseveres.

Love never fails.

1 CORINTHIANS 13:6–8 NIV

"I felt so loved when I had cancer," said Mary. "I had to trust in the love of God to get me through every day and to do what I needed to do. But He showed me that love through other people."

The love "just poured in" from friends, family, strangers, and other cancer survivors. They brought food to her house, did her laundry, brought music tapes and videos, and sent helpful cards.

"Some people will show love because they've been through cancer themselves or they're related to you," said Mary. "But other people just have the compassion of God—and some are looking to give back because they've received love at some time in the past. Whether people knew it or not, they all showed me God's love."

Mary believes the love of God, demonstrated to her by others, made her heal much more quickly than usual. "The doctors were amazed at how fast I healed. But the love didn't only work a physical healing. I was also emotionally healed. Because of all the love shown me, I was able to put the cancer experience behind me."

As an active leader in her church, for once Mary had to learn to sit back and let others do for her for a change. "Sickness is a time to simply allow ourselves to be loved and not worry about what else we're going to do," said Mary.

Is there someone near you who needs you to show her God's persistent love?

Dear children,
let us not love with words
or tongue but with
actions and in truth.

1 JOHN 3:18

Growing in Love

You can show God's supporting love to someone who is sick by...

- bringing a casserole or other main dish to the home. Buy some inexpensive baking dishes at rummage sales so the family won't have to worry about returning them.
- giving a tape or CD with praise and worship music. There is healing in worship.

- doing the laundry. Go to the person's house and get it, then take it to your home to wash and dry. Ask about special soaps that must be used and don't forget the clothes hangers.
- running errands—dry cleaner's, groceries, car wash, kids' music lesson, video store, etc.
- sharing a good video. This is no time for sad, die-at-the-end movies. Find truly funny ones or movies with happy endings.
- bringing a good book.
- temporarily assuming his or her duties. This might mean teaching a Sunday school class, attending a child's Little League game, or substituting as a Brownie leader.
- cleaning the house. Ask if you can come over and do the dishes, clean the bathrooms, or run the vacuum cleaner.
- not relaying bad news or gossip.
- reading aloud a favorite book or renting some books on tape.
- bringing a pretty nightgown or robe if it is a woman who is ill.
- praying with the person.

A HARVEST OF LOVE

Persistent Fruit That Heals Heartbreak
Life-Giving Love

"I made sure that no one knew," said Bill, "but I was planning to commit suicide." It was all planned and he was going to do it on Friday afternoon.

A lot of things had gone wrong in his life. His marriage was crumbling, he had lost his job, and he was facing financial ruin because of a business deal gone sour. "I always thought that no matter how tough life got, I could handle it. But when a lot of the bad things happened all at once, I started to fall apart," said Bill.

Then to make things worse, Bill's health started to fail. "I had the most excruciating backaches. They were so bad I'd be incapacitated for several days at a time. And I barely got any sleep. I could find no comfortable position."

A longtime Christian believer, when Bill prayed now, he felt as though the heavens had turned to brass and God wasn't listening. "Always before, I felt the presence of God in my life, but lately I felt like He had turned totally away from me and left me on my own. I know now that God heard every word; He was right there with me, but I just couldn't feel anything but pain. He wanted to show His love for me in a totally different way."

On Friday morning, Roger, a Christian friend from Bill's

church, called Bill and asked if he could take him out for coffee and a chat. "God must have laid me on Roger's heart, because we weren't exactly close before. The thing was, I was planning to kill myself that very afternoon. I had even made prearrangements at the local funeral home and put a note on the suit I was to be buried in. But for some reason I still don't quite understand, I did have coffee with Roger. I ended up pouring out my troubles to him, although I didn't tell him that I was planning to commit suicide.

"He just listened," said Bill. "When I was done, he said, 'Let me pray for you.' I thought he meant then, but he said, 'I have a group of men I pray with, and I'll tell them your problems without mentioning your name. We'll pray for you every day until the Lord answers.'

"When he said that, I thought, *I think I'll stick around for a few more days just to see what happens!*

"A few days later, I got a note in the mail from Roger. In it was a list of prayer requests these men were praying for me. Even though the list didn't mention my name, I was embarrassed to need so much prayer. But I soon got over that. I was curious to see what God was going to do!"

Bill is still amazed at how the Lord answered the specific prayer requests on that list. "I started dating the list when God answered this prayer or that, and then I'd show the list to Roger so his prayer group could thank God for the answers and concentrate on my other needs," said Bill. "Eventually, every request was answered. I framed that list and put it on my desk in my new office.

"I can't tell you how much it meant to me to have people faithfully praying for me. It literally saved my life."

Confess your faults one to another,
and pray one for another,
that ye may be healed.
The effectual fervent prayer of
a righteous man availeth much.
JAMES 5:16

For where two or three
are gathered together
in my name,
there am I in
the midst of them.

MATTHEW 18:20

A HARVEST OF LOVE

Sowing Persistent Love on Thorny, Rocky Ground
Praying Relentlessly for the Prodigal

Who is your prodigal?

He may be your child. Your mate. Your co-worker. Your friend. Your neighbor. You love him but he just won't listen to the gospel. He may have stopped listening to you altogether. In fact, you may not even know where he is.

As long as you have breath, keep praying for his repentance. Remember: It is not God's will that any should perish but that all should come to repentance (2 Peter 3:9), so you know when you pray for him, you are praying in God's will. This is a prayer God wants to answer, a prayer Jesus died to make a reality.

Trust God to answer. Your prodigal may not be reconciled to God in your lifetime, but Hebrews 11 relates the accounts of many people who trusted God for impossible things and received them—though not always during the span of their years on earth.

Consider fasting for a soul's salvation. When God's people humble themselves, confess their sins, and pray, He does mighty works for them. Read through the Bible, and you will see how God intervened for His people when they fasted and prayed.

Cultivating Faithful Love
A Lesson from a Father

"I learned about unconditional love from my father," said Carl.

Way back in 1923, when Carl was twelve years old, he needed some dental work done. While he sat in the chair sweating through a tooth extraction, the dentist and Carl's father discussed the Thompsons, a large family who attended their church.

The dentist, considered to be a religious man, was relating that one of the Thompsons' sons took their new car without permission and wrecked it. This was a great financial loss to the family.

"If that were my son," said the dentist, "I would tell him to get out and never come back. Wouldn't you?"

Carl has never forgotten his father's reply: "No, I tell my children that no matter what they have done, they can always come home."

"That's one of the ways I came to understand my heavenly Father's love," said Carl.

Love remains regardless of rebuke or reward.

Growing in Love Despite Harsh Conditions— Committed Love

Roberta's unemployed husband Jack is often impatient and volatile, but never more so than when he is sick. At those times, he lashes out at everyone around him. During Christmas break, when all of the children were home from school and Roberta's life was a whirl of activities, Jack came down with the flu.

"It's really too bad he didn't have laryngitis instead," said Roberta.

With the children close at hand, Jack ragged at them and Roberta about every little thing. He made everyone miserable.

"I sent the kids overnight to various neighbors and relatives, hoping that Jack would get well and be civil," said Roberta. "He didn't seem to realize how strange it was for him to be sitting up in bed reading his Bible while bellowing at the kids!"

Unfortunately, Jack's flu settled in his chest. The kids had to come home sometime, and Roberta realized they were all in for a long, nasty siege, which is precisely what happened.

Jack had a particular knack for verbally attacking people where they were the most vulnerable. Roberta cited an example: "I was doing laundry and things were a mess in the laundry room. Jack said, 'You and those kids have made this house into a pigsty!' He knew we had been cleaning and that I take pride in keeping the house tidy. He didn't want to clean the laundry room himself, but he wanted it clean right then.

"I was upset. What he said wasn't true. He just shot off his mouth for his own advantage.

"But I realized God is forcing me to bear fruit—such as unfailing love. If I'm really committed to Christ, I can't just say to Jack, 'Because you said that, my commitment to you is dissolved.' Even though some days I wish I could.

"I sometimes get so frustrated with Jack that I almost hate him and I'm ready to give up on the marriage. Then I come back to God, and it is my commitment to Him that makes me persevere. Satan would like me to focus on the things I don't like about Jack. We have some real problems that will only be solved over time, if at all. But when my anger passes, the love God puts in my heart enables me to continue to love Jack, despite his flaws.

"We all have flaws. Who knows? Maybe Jack struggles with the very same feelings I do, only about some flaw of mine that I don't realize. Thank goodness our commitment to each other is rooted in our commitment to Christ. God's love for me shows me how to love Jack. Part of forgiving is forgetting."

True love perseveres despite hardship. Sometimes our reward for loving in the face of trials comes soon; sometimes we must wait until eternity to see the harvest of the love we've sown.

A Prayer for
Good Growing Conditions

Dear Lord,

You know how hard it is for me to love sometimes, especially in the face of frustration or rejection. Enrich the soil of my heart with Your
Spirit; send the rain of Your grace to soften my
flinty soul; keep rooting out the weeds that choke
out the good growth. Help me to never give up on
others. Thank You that You never give up on me.

Chapter 16

Love Always Hopes
Planting Seeds of Hopeful Love

Love. . .

always hopes.

1 CORINTHIANS 13:6–7 NIV

The hope of the righteous shall be gladness.
PROVERBS 10:28

A definition:

- *Hope:* A feeling that what is wanted will happen.

Slow to Fruit—
Hoping Against Hope

It took Esther and Bob fourteen years before they could face the fact their son was brain damaged.

When they adopted him at birth, he looked so much like a normal baby that even the pediatrician didn't diagnose fetal alcohol effects. An unusually pretty baby and a quick learner, the family adored him, although he was cranky and hard to manage. Most difficult of all, he didn't connect his actions as the cause of rewards or discipline. When he was told "no" or his hands were slapped, he thought people were just being mean.

When he reached adolescence, his behaviors became more extreme and sometimes violent. Despite the fact that Bob and Esther had attempted to raise him up in the way he should go, despite the fact that they prayed and fasted one day a week for him, their son's misbehaviors eventually landed him in a detention facility.

"For many years, we prayed and asked God to send us a child. And then He did. He sent us our son," said Esther. "Well, God doesn't make mistakes. I believe somehow He will heal our son and use him for His glory. I don't know how; I don't have to know, but I know God does. I just cling to that."

Hope—
The Seedling of Faith

- Hope wishes to please God. Faith offers a meaningful sacrifice.
- Hope desires a relationship with God. Faith walks and talks with Him.
- Hope desires God's protection. Faith builds an ark.
- Hope wishes for a Promised Land. Faith follows God's directions to find it.
- Hope sees a child's potential. Faith helps a child achieve it.
- Hope desires to understand others. Faith spends time listening.
- Hope wishes for friendship. Faith meets the needs of others.
- Hope wants to provide for the family. Faith gets an education and works long hours.
- Hope aspires to rear godly children. Faith teaches them the Bible and leads by example.
- Hope yearns for peace. Faith works to achieve it.
- Hope looks to Jesus for forgiveness. Faith thanks Him for it and repents.
- Hope desires to see loved ones in heaven. Faith shows them the way to the Pearly Gates.

And without faith it is impossible to please God.
HEBREWS 11:6 NIV

The Fruit of Hope— A Life Rewritten by "Mr. P."

Born to an unwed teenage mother in Houston's Hispanic ghetto, Sal's future didn't look too promising. "We lived in a high-crime, low-rent neighborhood. We didn't know we were poor, because everybody around us was poor," said Sal.

When Sal's mother married, she chose an alcoholic. The man adopted Sal, but he never connected emotionally with Sal. "He was there," said Sal, "but he was pursuing liquor. He was not a father to me."

The neighborhood school where Sal attended was not known as a positive place either. Said Sal: "E–School was infamous for its violence and stabbings. It still is. It did not have a high standard of academics or discipline. This was in the early sixties, way before gangs were even talked about by the national media, but we had them at E." Sal even saw a fellow student shot between the eyes in the school hall.

With this as his background, Sal entered seventh grade and

the notorious no-man's-land of adolescence. His horizons were limited to the crime-ridden streets of the barrio, and his future seemed to be written in the profane graffiti on the walls—until he caught the attention of Mr. P., one of his schoolteachers.

A man with a secret sorrow (his fiancée had died in a car wreck), Mr. P. had never married and he had no biological children. He was a highly educated man who had once been offered a lucrative position as the editor of a major newspaper, but instead Mr. P. took on the responsibility of teaching journalism with missionary zeal to the inner-city children. Because Sal showed writing skills, he was one of six Hispanic boys admitted to Mr. P.'s class.

The curriculum for this class consisted of reporting and distributing the school newspaper. Mr. P. and the boys wrote the stories, shot and developed the photographs, sold ads to local businesses, ran the paper off on the mimeograph, and sold it in the school cafeteria.

"We were 'his' kids," said Sal. "He could see what we could become, but we could not. Actually, he was aiming low, just hoping to give us a little broader horizon, but the Holy Spirit had other plans. Mr. P. gave us much more than his teaching abilities; he gave us himself. He cared about his students and took on parental chores and responsibilities. He got involved in our families.

"Mr. P. would pile the whole group of us into his car and take us to the museum or a movie or a play. He introduced us to his church and encouraged us to go and become involved." It was through these experiences that Sal became a Christian.

This type of father-son interaction was just the relationship for which Sal had been searching. He clung to it, growing close to Mr. P.'s family, adopting their values. He began to believe that God really cared about him. When Sal went on to high school, like the other five boys in the journalism class, he kept in touch with Mr. P. When any of them needed guidance, they picked up the phone to ask Mr. P.

Through the ensuing years, Sal continued to turn to Mr. P. whenever he needed to make decisions. Mr. P.'s continued encouragement led Sal to earn a four-year degree, go to graduate school, become a teacher, then an elementary/middle-school principal. As a lay pastor, Mr. P. even took part in Sal's wedding ceremony.

The hopeful vision of Mr. P. has borne much fruit: Of the six boys in the journalism class, three have college degrees; all have meaningful careers. "I have a different lifestyle today because of Mr. P.," said Sal. "He provided the father figure I didn't have. I send him a card on Father's Day. If I need advice, he's still the one I call."

Hopeful love changes the world.

Planting the Seeds of Hope Through Prayer

Dear Lord,
Please plant in my heart
the seeds of hope.
May my love for others
always ever hope for their best.

Chapter 17

Unsurpassable Love
The Greatest of These Is Love—
A Seed That Will Never Die

And now
these three remain:
faith, hope and love.
But the greatest of these is love.

1 CORINTHIANS 13:13 NIV

It was a freak accident that electrocuted Lucy and Mark's son Brian when he was two years old. Fortunately, Mark was on hand to call the paramedics and begin CPR until they arrived. His quick thinking no doubt saved Brian's life.

Once at the hospital, Brian lay in a deep coma for several weeks. Scans indicated brain activity, but no one knew for sure how much damage had been done. Slowly, Brian returned to the land of the living, but over time it became apparent he had sustained severe damage to the area of the brain that controls motor movement. Doctors told Lucy and Mark that Brian would never walk or talk; he would be confined to a wheelchair all his remaining days.

Caring for Brian was a twenty-four-hour-a-day job, most of which fell to Lucy. The couple had other small children who also required attention.

"The Lord gave me extra grace at that time," said Lucy. "I was angry at God, but He was still faithful. His love never failed me."

While no one knew how much Brian understood about the world around him, Lucy and Mark stressed to their family that Brian should be included in conversations, not ignored like he "was a human-shaped vegetable in a wheelchair," said Lucy. Not only did they talk to him, however; they also read to him, prayed with him, and even included him in family games. Brian occasionally made noises and rolled his eyes, but they could never tell how much he was absorbing.

However, one day their loving patience paid off.

In the special classroom where the now fifteen-year-old Brian received his education, a specially adapted computer was set up for his use. By blinking, Brian could choose alphabet letters and form words. To everybody's amazement, Brian not only already knew the alphabet, but also could read, spell, and communicate. He already had a deep faith in Christ. He had been paying attention all along!

Brian's special friend at school was another boy, Nick, whose physical injuries were equal to Brian's in severity. However, Nick's emotional injuries were much more damaging. Abandoned by his parents shortly after his accident, Nick had been cared for by the state for more than ten years. Connected by computer, the two boys communicated with one another, and Nick's anguish and resentment poured out to Brian.

One day, Brian surprised his parents with a request: "Will you adopt Nick?" he blinked into his computer. With complete understanding of what caring for a profoundly damaged boy entailed, Lucy and Mark legally made Nick their son, too.

When people ask how they can possibly have enough love and patience to handle two such boys, Lucy and Mark have been heard to reply, "Love and patience are the same thing."

True love is bigger than any problem. It is the greatest thing in the world. Nothing can overcome it.

Jesus' love is bigger than any heartache.

Some people are far harder to love than others. But the love that comes from the Holy Spirit is supernatural. How the Holy Spirit generates love for the unlovely in many cases is nothing short of a miracle.

Thou shalt love thy neighbour as thyself:
I am the LORD.
LEVITICUS 19:18

Though I speak with tongues of men and of angels,
and have not charity, I am become as sounding brass,
or a tinkling cymbal.
And though I have the gift of prophecy,
and understand all mysteries, and all knowledge;
and though I have all faith, so that I could remove mountains,
and have not charity, I am nothing.
1 CORINTHIANS 13:1–2

A HARVEST OF LOVE

What many of us call love is really only some pretty emotion that's a mile wide and an inch deep. It covers the surface everyone can see—but it is only a pretty veneer. Beneath the surface is a heart that is rotten with selfishness and indifference.

The Power of Love

Dot was squarely built and she waddled back and forth when she walked like she was holding a bale of hay in each fist. She fettered her rolled-up hair under a net and had a *laissez faire* attitude about wearing her dentures.

As a widow with an adopted son who was something of a young hellion, Dot had her capable hands full at home, but she financially stretched the ends together by doing laundry at a local nursing home and working as the church janitor. In this capacity, we kids of the church knew her best and appreciated her the most.

While the adults were sagely deciding weighty matters during after-service meetings, we children had the run of the halls, basement, parking lot, and yard. Needless to say, we got our Sunday clothes stained, our stockings covered with beggar's-lice, and occasionally drew blood with bumps and scrapes. But we always found an ally in Dot.

She didn't scold about our messes or complain about some of the extra work we made for her. She also knew how to invisibly mend torn lace, remove mud spatters from small purses and anklets, and restore the polish to patent-leather shoes. On more than one occasion, she kept us from getting into serious trouble with our parents by bailing us out of a self-inflicted disaster. We appreciated her.

She understood what Jesus meant when He said, "Let the children come unto Me." She knew that if we considered the church our home we'd find it a good place to be both as youngsters and later as adults. She didn't have a lot of theological expertise, but she understood the basic principle of building a church: The church is made up of people and people make messes. You love the person and clean up the mess.

Who Is My Neighbor?

When Jesus was asked this question, He answered it with a story, the parable we know as "The Good Samaritan (Luke 10:30–36)." In the story, Jesus related the circumstances of a lone traveler who was waylaid by thieves, stripped and beaten, and left near death. After the fact, three people, a priest, a Levite, and a Samaritan, saw the traveler lying beside the road. Only one stopped to help him.

There are several facts you should know about this story:

- The road that stretched from Jerusalem to Jericho was a serpentine pathway notorious for the gangs of highwaymen who held up anyone who was so foolhardy to travel it alone.

- The traveler was a foolish man who was asking for trouble by traveling alone on such a dangerous highway. He had no one but himself to blame for his dilemma.

- The priest moved as far away from the injured man as he could. He knew that if he touched a dead body, he would be ritually unclean for seven days (Numbers 19:11) and unable to perform any of the temple rituals. He would not risk that. To him, ceremony was more important than charity; liturgy was elevated above anguish. He passed by without offering help.

- The Levite noticed the man and studied him from afar, but he knew that the hijackers often used a decoy to lure kindhearted travelers to let down their guard. The Levite had no intention of being caught in that trap. His own skin was too precious to risk. He, too, passed by without coming to the man's aid.

- The term "Samaritan" was a racial slur hurled at people who were considered heretics or villains. Jesus' listeners might have hissed at the mere mention of a Samaritan. But this man stopped to help the injured traveler. He took responsibility for a man who had brought his trouble upon himself.

Here is what we learn from Jesus' story:

- We must lovingly care for everyone—even those who have brought their troubles upon themselves.

- Our help must be of a practical nature. It is not enough to be sympathetic. Compassion and love are in freely doing, not in feeling.

Have you ever wondered what God sees when He looks at our hearts when we pray? Here's a peek inside a soul who does not understand who her neighbor truly is or what it means to love.

Dear Lord,

Lord, let my neighbors be powerful because they can wield influence for me, not the downtrodden because they are so needy that they can't do anything for me.

Let my neighbors be rich so they can help me lay up treasures on earth. Moths, rust, or thieves don't really worry me; tomorrow may not ever come. Don't let my neighbors be poor because they might cost me something.

Let my neighbors be the beautiful people because I'll be attractive by association. But I don't want the plain or deformed, sick or crippled, emotionally, mentally, or physically challenged people for my neighbors, because others will think something is wrong with me, too.

Let my neighbors be the popular crowd because I want to be where the action is. But don't let the quiet, in-the-background people be my neighbors. They won't be any fun at all.

Let my neighbors be worthy of my love. I want to help those who will be successful in the sight of everyone else—and then I can take credit for their success. If I help someone who is a wastrel, I might look like a fool.

And don't let my neighbors be time-consuming, because I have things I want to do for myself.

So please answer my prayer, Lord. I want to love my neighbor as myself and I think I'm better than most people.

Nothing is greater than love; we can ask for no better fruit to grow in our lives. Don't be content with the artificial kind, the kind of fake love demonstrated by this prayer. Instead, allow the Master Gardener to work the soil of your heart until the best growth of all springs forth, the growth for which you were created. You will be surprised by the fresh fragrance that love will spread throughout your life.

And though I bestow
all my goods to feed the poor,
and though I give
my body to be burned,
and have not charity,
it profiteth me nothing.

1 CORINTHIANS 13:3

A Prayer to the Master Gardener

Dear Lord,
Please sow the seeds of love in my life.
Nourish the young growth with Your Spirit's
blessing. Root out these weeds:

- *Envy*
- *Pride*
- *Pleasure in others' misfortunes*

- *Selfishness*
- *Anger*
- *Grudges*

And one day may my life yield a bountiful harvest of. . .

- *Patient love*
- *Loving-kindness*
- *Humility*
- *Selflessness*
- *Unconditional love*

- *Truthfulness*
- *Protection*
- *Trust*
- *Hope*
- *Persistence*

Beloved, let us love one another: for love is of God; and every one that loveth is born of God, and knoweth God. . . . for God is love.

1 JOHN 4:7–8

About the Author

Rebekah Montgomery has over thirty years of experience as a pastor and teacher. A prolific writer, she is the author of several books; many magazine, newspaper, and inspirational articles; camp and Bible school curriculum; and children's musicals. Rebekah is the author of *Ordinary Miracles: True Stories of an Extraordinary God Who Works in Our Everyday Lives* (Promise Press, May 2000), and is presently developing a book series on the *Fruit of the Spirit* (Promise Press, July 2000).

Rebekah lives in Kewanee, Illinois, with John, her husband of thirty years, and their three children, Mary, Joel, and Daniel.